Inside Family Viewing

Against a backdrop of growing unease with traditional quantitative empirical research methods and an equal unease with abstract psychoanalytic models, ethnography is increasingly seen as one of the few empirical methods that is not undercut by contemporary theoretical work. Indeed, it is only recently that ethnography has begun to show its ability to describe and explain phenomena in media studies. James Lull's work in this area has proved to be an influential model. This collection presents rich accounts of how television intersects with family life in American and other world cultures. It will be of interest not only to those in media and communications, but also to those in the broader fields of cultural anthropology and sociology.

James Lull is a researcher, writer, and broadcaster who lives in San Francisco, California. He is editor of *Popular Music and Communication* (Sage Publications, 1987) and *World Families Watch Television* (Sage Publications, 1988). His most recent work is *China Turned On: Television, Reform and Resistance* (Routledge, forthcoming), an ethnographic study of television's role in the troubled development of the People's Republic of China.

D1067149

Comedia
Series editor: David Morley

Inside Family Viewing

Ethnographic Research on
Television's Audiences

James Lull

A Comedia book
published by Routledge
London and New York

A Comedia book

First published 1990
by Routledge
11 New Fetter Lane, London EC4P 4EE

Simultaneously published in the USA and Canada
by Routledge
a division of Routledge, Chapman and Hall, Inc.
29 West 35th Street, New York, NY 10001

© 1990 James Lull

Phototypeset in 10/12pt Times by
Input Typesetting Ltd, London

Printed in Great Britain by
Clays Ltd., St. Ives plc

British Library Cataloguing in Publication Data
Lull, James
  Inside family viewing: ethnographic research on television's audience.
  1. Family life. Role of television
  I. Title
  306.85

Library of Congress Cataloging-in-Publication Data
Lull, James.
    Inside family viewing: ethnographic research on television's audience
  / James Lull.
      p.   cm. – (Comedia)
    Includes bibliographical references.
    1. Television and family—Cross-cultural
studies.   I. Title.   II. Series.
  HQ520.L85 1990
  306.8′5—dc20   90–32941
                                              CIP

ISBN 0–415–04414–6
ISBN 0–415–04997–0 pbk

For my mother, Verna Marie Lull

Contents

List of tables

Preface

The appearance of this collection of James Lull's work over the last ten years marks an important stage in the study of the role of the mass media in contemporary culture. For some years the development of media research in quantitative and qualitative sociology and in cultural studies has been held back by a lack of dialogue across these different traditions. As so often, researchers within each field have been most concerned with their (often, in relative terms, small) differences with others working within their own problematic. In terms of book publishing, journals and conferences each different tradition has largely kept to its own and, in consequence, these debates have often been unhelpfully isolated from each other. If this isolation has occurred within each national academic community it has been exacerbated as between researchers in Britain and the United States (with, of course, some honourable exceptions).

In recent years North American researchers, such as Lull, working from a qualitative sociological tradition, have become increasingly interested in the (principally British) cultural studies tradition. Their interest in that work, and their attempts to develop it in the context of their own qualitative research, have been an important first step in constructing a potentially valuable dialogue. However, much of this more recent North American work is neither widely known nor readily available outside its home territory. Indeed Lull's essays collected here have been hard to get hold of in Britain, scattered as they are throughout a number of different North American journals. Their publication in this volume will hopefully stimulate a greater awareness of this contemporary North American work, in Britain and elsewhere.

In recent years, media researchers in Britain (myself included) have become increasingly aware of the need to understand the domestic context of television use and consumption. Lull's work constitutes a valuable resource for all those concerned with this recent (and continuing) phase of development in media audience research. In particular, Lull's contribution to ethnomethodological and ethnographic research in this field is, in my view, of greatest interest. Lull himself speaks of the current influence in North American communications and media studies of the work of the Birmingham Centre for Contemporary Cultural Studies. In that context it is worth noting that, despite a passing engagement with ethnomethodological perspectives in the early 1970s and the subsequent production of some work (Willis 1977; Hebdige 1979; Hobson 1982) within a loosely ethnographic frame, this was one possible research trajectory which remained underdeveloped in the work of CCCS. In Lull's work the insights into micro-processes which ethnomethodological and ethnographic perspectives allow in empirical research are powerfully demonstrated.

Lastly, as one whose own work has been influenced by Lull, I have to declare my interest. I hope that readers of this collection will come to share that interest.

DAVID MORLEY
London

Acknowledgments

This book represents much of what I have produced in my academic career during the past ten years, work that has benefited greatly from many people. It is tempting to try to thank them all. But any list of personal acknowledgments constructed here surely would be incomplete. Instead, I would like to single out and thank four people whose intellectual vitality and personal kindness have been central to my work and to my life.

When I began graduate school at the University of Oregon in 1971, I had the good fortune to meet Professor Glenn Starlin. Glenn's gentle, unpretentious, fatherly prodding, his personal encouragement and support, his insights and enthusiasm for the field were just what I needed at the time. I will always hold in my heart the greatest respect and admiration for Glenn Starlin, my master's degree advisor.

My graduate education continued at the University of Wisconsin. The chairman of the Department of Communication Arts and editor of the *Quarterly Journal of Speech* at the time was Professor Edwin Black. Ed Black directed my doctoral dissertation, 'Mass Media and Family Communication: An Ethnography of Audience Behavior', and encouraged me to pursue the line of work that is represented in this volume. Ed Black is the consummate scholar and teacher, someone whose example will live with me always.

When I was an undergraduate student at San Jose State University in the late 1960s and early 1970s, I met a young professor of Communication Studies who years later would become my close personal friend and most valued colleague. Phil Wander truly has been a mentor for me. He has taught me more about communication, politics, and culture than anyone. It is simply not possible to have a better colleague. Phil's stimulating intellectualism is matched by his genuine liberalism, his sensitivity and deep concern for others – all of which has touched me deeply.

Finally, I want to thank Ien Ang, who teaches Communication Studies at the University of Amsterdam, Holland. More than anyone, Ien has helped me understand the importance of cultural studies theory and research. Her demanding, precise intellectual style is the sharp side; the sensitive, supportive, yet crazy and fun-loving personality is the soft side of this wonderful scholar and remarkable woman.

Thanks, Glenn, Ed, Phil, and Ien.

JAMES LULL
San Francisco

1 An emerging tradition: ethnographic research on television audiences*

As a military journalist in Vietnam in 1965 and 1966, I wrote stories about what it meant to fight that grinding, awful war. The articles described what American men encountered, moment by moment, in the torments and labors of fighting. The stories were about men like Pat Stephens, a radio-telephone operator who carried the bulky communications equipment for a year only to watch his replacement killed by a Viet Cong sniper bullet just hours after Pat passed the radio to him. I wrote about Derrick Brase, a 17-year-old farm kid from my home state of Minnesota who lost his life fighting for reasons that were completely unclear to him. I described my own feelings the first time I saw a man killed and I wrote about how Frank Quinto handled waiting in line at the medical tent with a bullet hole in his back. I wrote about the depression that came when the troops could not get dry for weeks during the monsoon rains. I told of a young soldier's frustration and sadness when he found out that the crying woman whose worldly possessions he had carried on his back all day on the way to an American 'protection zone' simply wanted to return to the little village where the trip had started – the place where her husband, a Viet Cong, was waiting.

I can still see the faces of these people and hear their voices. I can still smell the jungle and taste the C-rations, though the war now seems to have been fought a million years ago. In Vietnam I wanted to tell stories that were not revealed in the body counts and official rationalizations of military press briefings. The war was fought far more personally than that.

It is a harsh, even disturbing comparison, but the official language

*I would like to thank Ien Ang, Phil Wander, David Morley, Tom Lindlof, Michelle Wolf, and Larry Wenner for their comments on an earlier draft of this chapter.

of the military in Vietnam and the official language of social science, and I refer here specifically to the quantitative science of communication studies in America, are limited in similar ways. It is a cold, detached language that is used to create, manipulate, and analyze *categories* of things. The categories, whether expressed through words or mathematical symbols, become the bases for inference.

But these are not the only alternatives. Just as journalistic investigative reports can describe and explain news events, qualitative empirical work conducted within academic disciplines can describe and explain social conditions and processes. Whether the subject is how people cope with war in the discomforts of a far-off land, or how families watch television programs in the comforts of their homes, the principle of qualitative empirical research is clear: to know the subjects you are analyzing requires intimate and sustained contact with them. This requires a research strategy that enables the researcher to enter into the life-space of human subjects and get to know them on their own terms. In my view, qualitative empirical research responds well to this requirement.

Now, more than twenty years after leaving Vietnam, I realize that the reporting style I developed as a young military journalist has greatly influenced my academic research and writing. In this introduction to the collection of articles that follows, I will describe several other key events and influences in the development of my research and writing about television audiences. I will do this by first examining central aspects of a larger picture – the development of communication studies and communication science in the United States and their relation to other traditions, British cultural studies in particular.

COMMUNICATION STUDIES AND COMMUNICATION SCIENCE IN THE UNITED STATES

With some notable exceptions, nearly every college campus in the United States has a communication studies department of some sort.[1] Many have two or three closely-related departments with communication at the core: mass communication, journalism, linguistics, speech, broadcasting, and rhetoric are among them. Fueled by students' widespread concern about the job market in the 'information age', communication is one of the true growth areas in American higher education. But the pervasiveness and ambiguousness of communication as an academic discipline have also led to unsteadiness and fragmentation. Communication studies departments frequently alter their curricula and change their names (for example, from 'speech' to 'speech-communication' to 'communication arts and sciences' to 'communication studies', and so on). These may be necessary adaptations in such a pragmatic and dynamic field, but they are modifications that have often created images of instability in the typically conservative, slow-moving academic environment.

Even more problematic is the fact that, except for the study of rhetoric, the field does not have a long-standing or respected intellectual lineage. Communication studies' central areas of scholarly inquiry in the modern era – interpersonal, mediated, and intercultural communication – have research traditions that are far less well developed than those of most other disciplines. Furthermore, nearly every emphasis within communication studies is rooted in practical skills training, an orientation that also generates a poor image for the field on campus. Given all these difficulties, communication scholars sometimes argue about how to improve the position of communication studies in the American academy.

Some scholars believe that scientific research and theorizing that is based on collection of quantitative data can help communication studies legitimize its place in academe. But over the years these efforts have encountered serious difficulties. Simply put, human communication activity often eludes scientific methodology. Many aspects of artistic texts and the complex processes of social interaction resist parsimonious and 'objective' assessments. None the less, methodologies based on hypothetico-deductive logic and quantification have been widely adopted in communication studies. The field has been dominated by social scientific theory and research since the late 1950s. Even today communication studies' identity is shaped largely by the scientific component despite its failure to produce many exciting theoretical insights.

The roots of communication science

The pioneering scientific research on communications phenomena in the United States was done in departments and institutes of psychology and sociology. The first empirical studies of persuasion and attitude change, language, public opinion, learning theory, media socialization, cognitive processing, and interpersonal relations, for example, were not done by communication scholars. The field's 'founding fathers', in the words of Wilbur Schramm (1963), were two psychologists (Kurt Lewin and Carl Hovland), a sociologist (Paul Lazarsfeld), and a political scientist (Harold Lasswell). Understandably, the field is widely considered to be a derivative or secondary *scientific* discipline. In fact, Schramm (1963) argued that communication studies became a field only when scientific research methods were introduced for study of communications phenomena and the resulting types of theory were advanced, developments that took place long after psychology and sociology had found their niches as social sciences in the academy. The 'latecomer' development of communication studies, its fragmented and unstable disciplinary status, its uncertainty about appropriate research methodologies, and its notable lack of important theories and theorists have all contributed to an unresolved identity crisis in the field.

The 1980s was the decade of great introspection within the communications field in the United States. Debates over the disciplinary and scientific status of the field appeared. A special issue of the *Journal of Communication* in 1983, subtitled 'Ferment in the Field', was the most ambitious and controversial stock-taking. Forty communication scholars assessed the maturity and promise of the field. Views ranged from Robert Stevenson's faith that 'the natural sciences can serve as models and guides for a true science of human behavior' (Stevenson 1983: 269) to Cees Hamelink's assertion that communication research should be about the 'emancipation' of the human race and that art serves this purpose much better than does science (Hamelink, 1983).

More recent commentaries appear in the *Handbook of Communication Science* edited by Charles Berger and Steven Chaffee. In their introduction to the book, the editors are encouraged that 'communication science' (and, by implication, 'communication studies') seems now to be less reliant on 'other fields for ideas' (Berger and Chaffee 1987: 16), a dubious accomplishment given the obvious multidisciplinary nature of human communication. The 'field' envisioned by scholars such as these is typically limited to its quantitative scientific element. Berger and Chaffee, for instance, to their credit claim that communication 'needs to be studied using methodologies that do not rely [only] upon a statistical approach'. But they define communication research as a 'science' that searches for 'lawful generalizations' in its theory building (p. 17), thereby ruling out many major streams of contemporary communication research, including some of the most successful and most promising varieties. The dominant theme here is territoriality – us versus them – at two levels: the independence of the communication discipline from other disciplines in the social sciences, and, within communication studies, the privileged status of quantitative research methods and quantitative scholars.

Ironically, this struggle over disciplinary and scientific legitimacy runs contrary to some of the best advice we are now getting from leading scholars in our parent disciplines. Herbert Gans, in his recent presidential address to the American Sociological Association, for example, challenged his colleagues to reach out to other disciplines, including the humanities, in the development of research and theory (Gans 1989). He called for deeper thinking ('thick analyses') and less methodological tinkering. He criticized the tendency toward 'overquantification', the futile search for sociological laws, and the uncritical way in which nomothetic sociology proceeds generally (Gans 1989). A similar, even more elaborate critique appears in Brenda Dervin *et al.*'s recent symposium *Rethinking Communication* (1989).

BRITISH CULTURAL STUDIES

Scientific communication research produced in the United States tends to be of a certain type and its practitioners follow explicit, standard methodological procedures. Despite these uniformities, American communication science is not really a community, a key difference from the other main contributor to contemporary research in communication and culture considered here, British cultural studies. Cultural studies has an even shorter history that is marked by a series of intellectual developments originally formulated by a small but highly influential group of scholars who, especially at the beginning, lived and worked in the same city. There is a much tighter correspondence between the 'discipline' of cultural studies and its theoretical and methodological underpinnings than is the case in communication studies.

Cultural studies' origins can be traced to the founding of a postgraduate research center at the University of Birmingham by Richard Hoggart in 1964. Stuart Hall directed the center from 1968 to 1981, and it is the work produced during this period, including especially the inspiring theoretical visions of Hall himself, that is most relevant to the study of mass media and culture. Unlike the uneven development of research and theory in American communication studies, the Birmingham center was an organizational hub for similar efforts in England. Furthermore, there was an explicit political component grounded in Marxism. By comparison, the functionalist bent of American communication science was for the most part unconsciously absorbed into research practices and was not explicitly political.[2]

Hall claims that there was no political or theoretical 'orthodoxy' at the Birmingham center, and that the research undertaken there was conducted in a democractic, non-dogmatic atmosphere (Hall 1980a).[3] None the less, Marxism is the reference point with which work produced at the center was considered and compared. Theoretical positions developing in Birmingham that were at odds with Marxist orthodoxy were considered evidence of 'open Marxism' or, especially with the concrete and celebrated theoretical development of ideological hegemony, of 'complex Marxism'.

Still, as Hall correctly claims, significant forays were made away from Marxist traditions. Not only was the model of economic determinism rejected, ideological determinism and its corresponding preoccupation with media texts as sole 'producers' or 'constructors' of meaning for audiences was made problematic. David Morley, a researcher at the center in the late 1970s, for instance, in a carefully worded key move takes issue with '*Screen* theory' – a theoretical position that focuses critically on media texts and treats viewer responses to media as predetermined (Morley 1980a). He argues that texts are 'polysemic' and that 'other texts and discourses' further influence audience 'readings'. He calls attention to the influence of social and cultural factors (reception contexts), especially the impact of gender and domestic relations on patterns of media reception.

Morley allows that television programs and other media texts contain 'preferred readings' consistent with dominant ideological visions, but he argues that audience interpretations are not limited to positions 'inscribed' in the text. Much of Morley's ground-breaking empirical work, especially *The 'Nationwide' Audience* (1980b) and *Family Television* (1986), reveals the complexities and validity of his theoretical argument. He describes not only the diversity of interpretations that audiences make of texts, but also many subtle uses to which media are put (a key conceptual overlap with my own work) as they take place within domestic family relations. In the end, Morley analyzes modes of television viewing as they are mediated by gender relations – produced through gender-specific patterns of socialization and the acting out of domestic roles – set within different socioeconomic class positions.

Many streams of contemporary European theory have influenced the Birmingham school. Cultural codes and practices were analyzed along the lines of structural linguistics (e.g. Claude Lévi-Strauss) and semiotics (e.g. Roland Barthes). Althusserian structuralist Marxism became a major influence, providing a framework for consideration of ideology that moved away from the outworn perspective of economic determinism. The 'discursive practices' of Michel Foucault provided a theoretical frame of reference that buttressed the argument of indeterminacy between ideology and social reality, offering a wider view of the exercise of social and cultural power. Lacanian psychoanalysis found a position in the Birmingham center's discourse about subjectivity and culture. 'Profound and unstoppable' feminism (Hall 1980a: 39) was credited as the ultimate critical cross-check on work done at the center. It proved to be a fresh theoretical resource that displaced forever any exclusive reference to class contradictions for cultural analysis.

The pre-eminent theoretical contribution to cultural studies, however, came from elaborations of Antonio Gramsci's theory of ideological hegemony. Properly fitted 'within the basic terms of a materialist theory' (Hall 1989a: 36) hegemony is a construct encompassing factors central to cultural studies' theorizing: culture and ideology placed in relation to economic and social class, a focus on *processes* of ideological influence, historical specificity, a concept of social power that is dynamic and open-ended, and a social theory that is appropriate for study of advanced industrial societies like the United Kingdom (Hall 1980a).[4] Hall's own writing about hegemony, wherein Gramsci's argument informs and is informed by communication theory (see e.g. Hall 1979, 1980b, 1986), is an insightful and enduring theoretical contribution to British cultural studies and to communication studies in general.

Despite its substantial contributions, British cultural studies can reasonably be criticized, in Hall's words, for its 'theoreticism', its preference for theory in place of 'concrete studies'. Indeed, when revisionist strains of Marxist theory entered into media studies at Birmingham, promoting, for example, analysis of the cultural implications of ideology, the polysemic nature of texts, and the variable contexts of reception, questions arose about how to study these new problematics. Most cultural studies researchers had self-consciously rejected mainstream American-style empiricist sociology from the beginning. Hypothetico-deductive research strategies that 'test' (functionalist-based) theories were likewise considered inappropriate. But the expansion of cultural studies into the new empirical areas demanded new research strategies. The focus of much cultural studies research had shifted away from modes of media production and textual analysis toward the interpretive and utilitarian activities of audience members as they are positioned within the contingencies of everyday life. A major figure at the Birmingham center, Paul Willis, put it this way: 'We are still in need of a method which respects evidence, seeks corroboration and minimizes distortion, but which is without the rationalist natural-science-like pretence' (Willis 1980: 91).

A suitable strategy was found. The prototypical empirical research practices for the study of media audiences within cultural studies were, and are, variations of ethnography. Ethnographic research undertaken by cultural studies scholars, like much of the material presented in the remaining chapters of this collection, requires direct contact with research subjects through 'participant observation' and/or depth interviewing. The decision to study cultural life in this way has not been without its problems for cultural studies theorists, opposed as most of them have been to employing methodological options that are in any way identified with the social sciences which, of course, ethnography is. According to Willis, even ethnography ultimately turns research 'subjects' into 'objects', an ideological conversion that is at odds with the philosophical and political biases of British cultural studies. Despite this problem, ethnography was adopted as an empirical research strategy at Birmingham and several cultural researchers at the center, including Dick Hebdige, Paul Willis, Dorothy Hobson, Phil Cohen, Roger Grimshaw, and David Morley have productively used ethnographic techniques in their accounts of cultural life in the United Kingdom.

The influence of British cultural studies extends well beyond the United Kingdom. It has become an important alternative to research produced within mainstream communication science. Many scholars in Europe, Australia (many of them British citizens), and North America have developed theoretical and empirical work inspired by the Birmingham research center. Furthermore, the publisher of this book, Routledge – especially through its subsidiary companies, Methuen and Comedia – has advanced work done in cultural studies by publishing numerous representative volumes.

ETHNOGRAPHIC STUDIES OF FAMILY VIEWING: THE EVOLUTION OF A RESEARCH PERSPECTIVE

Now, I would like to tell a more personal story in order to illustrate how I developed the work that comprises this volume. I have been influenced by both traditions discussed above. As a graduate student, I was trained by communication scientists, most of whom were not at all sympathetic to ethnographic research. Still, I was determined to write a doctoral dissertation about family television viewing that was based on ethnographic data. I will trace specific influences that encouraged me along the way, and recount some of the struggles that ensued. More recently, however, my inspiration has come from cultural studies. So, in the next sections of this chapter I will address some central issues concerning qualitative empirical audience research that impinge upon work now being done by scholars who represent both communication studies and cultural studies.

Doing graduate school

One requirement of graduate students at major institutions in the United States is completion of a series of courses in research methodology. At the University of Wisconsin – where I was a doctoral student in the middle 1970s – this meant enrolling in courses in research design, statistics, and computer science. Students who did not pursue a social science approach to their studies – those in rhetorical or film studies, for instance – could fulfill this requirement with coursework thought to be more appropriate to their emphasis – foreign languages, for example.

But by the mid-1970s quantitative research methodologies had reached their peak in the United States and were popularly considered, even by non-practitioners, to be the *ne plus ultra* of scholarship in our discipline. Quantification and statistical comparison of conceptual 'variables' was promoted as the most systematic means available to study interpersonal and mass communication, areas that had eclipsed rhetoric and public address as the definitive subjects of the field. Graduate students who elected to fulfill the methodology requirement some way other than through courses in scientific quantitative methods and statistics were thought to be unwilling, or, more likely, unable to do the tough work.[5] Learning to use statistics was the core ritual in the rites of passage for graduate students in communication studies. If you were clever with path analysis, sequential lag analysis, and multiple discriminant analysis, *you were a good student*. Other than the historical and literary methodologies assigned to rhetorical analysis, there seemed to be no alternatives to the growing fascination with social science.

I, too, was excited by the challenge to learn and apply statistical techniques to the study of communication events and processes. I went along with the idea that mastering research design, statistics, and the language of scientific writing was the way to become a communications researcher and qualify to teach at the college level. In fact, some of the most influential professors at Wisconsin and elsewhere were known mainly for their quantitative methodological contributions to the field. Their authority sprang from methodological competence. Arguments about the quality of communication research often centered much more on the fine points of methodological applications than on the substance of the work itself. At the time, Michigan State University was our field's 'in' graduate school, a distinction it earned mainly because of its enthusiastic adherence to the principles of scientific inquiry and quantitative methods of research. The dean and faculty of the School of Communication at Michigan State sought, as Everett Rogers points out, actually to determine the content of the field (Rogers and Chaffee 1983: 21).

With so many professors enamored by the nuances of quantitative methodologies, graduate students everywhere were trained in the operations of scientific methodology above all else. Such mechanical precision in measurement was necessary, according to one famous professor at Wisconsin, because communication is the study of 'human machines locked in interaction'. For many of us, then, the study of human communication was actually defined by our training in quantitative methodology – not theory, not politics, not criticism.

Relying on the range of techniques prescribed within the purview of science to 'solve problems' in communication promotes a stultifying conformist mentality. Mathematical 'proof' can be summoned to verify the logic of each statistical test. Human behavior is considered to be lawful. The challenge for the communication scientist, then, is to employ the proper test in order to discover predictable, lawful regularities in communication. Originality is discouraged when it poses questions or considers contexts that are not readily addressable by the stock of methodological tools. I'll never forget the roar of laughter I received in a research design course I was taking at Wisconsin when we discussed how to do research on the feelings that women have during the moment of childbirth. The 'correct' approach was to design a survey questionnaire where respondents were to indicate their degree of agreement or disagreement with pre-structured descriptions of what it is like to give birth. As an alternative, I suggested that researchers could videotape the faces of women as they gave birth, then play the tapes back for them later and ask them to describe their feelings. At the time, such a suggestion was beyond the range of the imaginable.

At about the same time, the mid-1970s, I was doing some reading that influenced me greatly.

The qualitative empirical alternative

Most important to me was Harold Garfinkel's smart and amusing work, *Studies in Ethnomethodology* (1967), a major breakthrough in American sociology that draws philosophically from Edmund Husserl's humanistic phenomenology and Alfred Schutz's theory of social intersubjectivity. Ethnomethods are the common, often taken-for-granted actions that people construct in order to organize and make meaningful the most routine aspects of everyday life. The ethnomethodological approach focuses on how social actors accomplish these fundamental operations of everyday life, including, of course, the construction of routine communication activity.

Any human behavior can be considered ethnomethodologically: walking, talking, viewing television. Each of these activities has a grammar in much the same sense as language does (Churchill 1971). The overarching theoretical position of ethnomethodology is that of a universal paradigm. Ethnomethodology encourages 'immaculate description of the case' in order to provide evidence of far-reaching 'generic social processes' (Lester and Hadden 1980) and explanations of the 'fundamental bases of social order' (Zimmerman 1978: 12).

Ethnomethodologists study concrete, social behavior – the 'practices that structure everyday life' (Mehan and Wood 1975: 17). But how can this kind of evidence be collected in order to formulate communication, mass communication, or cultural theory? More specifically, how can families, the most common viewing group, be studied in such detail?

Shortly after my introduction to Garfinkel's work, I read Oscar Lewis' classic cultural ethnographies of family life, *La Vida* (1965) and *Five Families* (1959), and Jules Henry's *Pathways to Madness* (1965), an ethnographic account of five mentally disturbed families. I discovered that there is a tradition of qualitative empirical work on family life that dates back before the turn of the last century. The in-home observational research of Pierre LePlay in France (1895), of Charles Booth in the United Kingdom (1970; his notebooks were published years after his death), and of W. I. Thomas and Florian Znaniecki in Europe and the United States (1918–20), is the best early work in this tradition. The famous qualitative empirical tradition in sociology was building at the University of

Chicago in the early decades of this century. Families were among the most common subjects for research, and the 'modal method' of the Chicago school was participant observation (LaRossa 1988). In England, 'mass observational' studies of families were conducted in the 1930s and 1940s. So, there certainly were precedents for doing ethnographic studies of families. Unfortunately, these qualitative, empirical options were virtually unheard of, and certainly not practiced, in communication studies at the time.

Applying ethnography to family viewing practices

My goals were to describe and explain how families interpersonally construct their time with television (and later, video) and how the medium intervenes in other aspects of communication activity at home and elsewhere. I was convinced that one of the most promising ways to study mass communication processes was to look at the details of interpersonal interaction. In fact, for precisely this reason I pursued a doctoral degree in communication theory that emphasized interpersonal communication, not mass communication.

Although the disciplinary structures of most American universities kept the study of mass communication and interpersonal communication separate, some key literature that appeared in the 1960s and 1970s encouraged integration. For instance, Herbert Blumer, the University of California sociologist instrumental in the development of 'symbolic interactionism', called for empirical research that fuses interpersonal and mass communication processes rather than considering 'each form or channel . . . as a distinct influence that can be kept separate and measured in some parallelogram of forces' (Blumer 1969: 187). In a similar spirit, American anthropologist Dell Hymes published the highly influential theoretical piece, 'Toward Ethnographies of Communication', in 1964. He outlined the importance of considering '[the] multiple hierarchy of relations among messages and contexts' in communication research, focusing on rules and processes more than on discrete elements of communication activity. Qualitative empiricism also formed the basis of Erving Goffman's famous theoretical work on interpersonal and 'public' communication (e.g. Goffman 1959, 1967, 1969). Both Hymes, an anthropologist, and Goffman, a sociologist, were faculty members at the University of Pennsylvania, a campus where ethnography and cultural analysis was also theorized and taught by Raymond Birdwhistell and Sol Worth, among others, at the Annenberg School of Communications. During the same period, 'grounded theory' was advanced by Barney Glaser and Anselm Strauss (1967) as a viable approach to theory construction using qualitative empirical research procedures.

The books discussed above and the type of material they contain were not presented in courses I took in graduate school. I really had two simultaneous graduate educations: the one that filled the requirements and the one I cooked up myself, the one that would contribute to the work represented in this volume.[6] Today, things may be changing somewhat.

QUALITATIVE EMPIRICAL RESEARCH ON TELEVISION'S AUDIENCES

Just as many American communication studies researchers once turned away from the field's qualitative roots in rhetoric and broadcasting, now some members of a new generation of scholars are questioning the indiscriminate use of quantitative research methods. A qualitative perspective is again beginning to emerge in a current wave of empirical media audience studies and theory building. In the United States, Thomas Lindlof's edited volume, *Natural Audiences: Qualitative Research of Media Uses and Effects* (1987) and my own collection, *World Families Watch Television* (1988) are among the new data-based qualitative projects. James Anderson and Timothy Meyer (1988) have written an advanced communication studies textbook that promotes 'accommodation theory', wherein the qualitatively assessed routines of everyday life are a key feature of the 'social action perspective' on communication that they advocate. Anderson, who has been a key contributor to the methodological debates in the United States for more than ten years, has also given prominence to qualitative empirical techniques in his recent methodology textbook (1987). Furthermore, many journal articles featuring qualitative empirical research in the study of media audiences have appeared during the past decade, including some special issues devoted exclusively to this type of work. I will not mention these individual studies here. Many of them are cited in the articles that follow.

Major research projects undertaken by Ien Ang (1985), David Morley (1986), Janice Radway (1984) – each with a distinct feminist orientation – and others reflect a simultaneous trend toward empirical audience research taking place in cultural studies. At the same time, a new strain of European *reception studies* is emerging that considers 'readers' (viewers) prominently in the analysis, rejecting the textual determinism of traditional Marxist and structuralist/ semiotic orientations that have influenced Europe's intellectual community for so many years. Klaus Bruhn Jensen of Denmark has helped lead the way with empirical research and theorizing in the new style of reception analysis (Jensen 1986, 1987, 1988), and has recently argued intriguingly for a 'social semiotics' of reception (Jensen, forthcoming).[7]

What unifies this partial convergence of traditions is a common interest in the qualitative features and processes of communication activity, especially the interpretations and uses of mass media that are constructed by audience members. This shared research agenda has helped gradually to break down distinctions historically held between mass and interpersonal communication, empirical and critical research, textual and audience studies, communication and cultural theory. I am indeed very enthusiastic about what this trend has produced and what it holds for the future. Still, a number of crucial issues may inhibit further integration.

THE POLITICS OF RESEARCH

Most important is the matter of politics. As discussed briefly earlier, the ideology of American communication science is built into and concealed by the assumptions that underlie its conduct. The political agenda of cultural studies, on the other hand, is far more transparent and self-consciously critical. Capitalism, racism, and patriarchy are the targets. Moreover, communication scientists typically believe that their methodological procedures excise politics and other 'contaminants' from the objective search for 'truth'. Some cultural studies scholars, on the other hand, sense the dominant position of scientific research in the formation of public policy and consider communication research itself a 'site of struggle' in a battle for political influence (e.g. Ang 1989).

Macro and micro issues in communication theory

The frequent explicit political formulations found within cultural studies research and theorizing reveal another key difference from most work done within communication science. Cultural studies theorists are generally far more attentive to the 'macro' issues in communication theory – the political, economic, ideological, and cultural factors. To their great credit, cultural studies scholars generally attempt to link everyday communication processes to macrosocial conditions; to show how the construction of culture is both enabled and limited within specific structural conditions.

Simply raising the 'big issues' in communication theory is itself a critical process, something that is almost always missing in American communication science research. Consider, for example, the empirically oriented journals of the two largest American communication organizations, *Communication Monographs* (published by the Speech Communication Association) and *Human Communication Research* (published by the International Communication Association). Editors of these journals still privilege quantitative method over all else. As a result, work published in these journals tends to be narrow, jargon-filled, scientistic accounts that rarely relate their empirical findings to macro issues.[8] 'Theory' is considered in the least powerful sense by relating this tiny study to that one, with occasional overviews of the tiny study literature. The work is not widely read, is rarely cited, and has had little impact outside the academy. Claims made for this type of research during the 1960s and 1970s, linking it with 'pure' research in the natural sciences, have collapsed. Despite these problems, much scientific work finds its inspiration and support in funding agencies for whom the appearance of rigor (i.e. quantification) still confers legitimacy and offers rewards. All of this is not an innocent process. As James Carey has observed, the positivist sciences have become 'part of the actual social process by which ideological forms mark and sustain the social order' (Carey 1985: 31).

Communication science does not need to be so limited in scope. George Gerbner and his colleagues at the University of Pennsylvania, for instance, have shown the critical potential of positivistic research. Their 'cultural indicators' project clearly shows how quantitative, empirical research can contribute to far more commentative analyses of the role of communication than is typically presented in scientific journals and books.

Critical attention to macro issues in American communication studies also informs the work of political economists such as Dallas Smythe, Herb Schiller, and others who have followed in their path. Unfortunately, political economic theory has not considered the empirical life-worlds of media audiences. Like early British cultural studies and European reception analysis, political economic theory in the United States and elsewhere was developed within the useful, but theoretically limiting framework of classical Marxism. Political economists identify the institutional origins and ideological impact of information flows throughout the world, but along the way media audiences have been characterized as passive recipients of messages and robotic reproducers of economic and cultural domination, an incomplete picture of reception and use.

Some recent cultural studies research, on the other hand, actively takes up the question of 'the audience', considering its roles in how meaning is constructed. Giving the audience a 'voice' has produced tangible, positive results. It has tempered the often pretentious and opaque writing associated with cultural studies, the frequent imposition of privileged interpretations of texts, a reliance on fashionable literature, and the dogmatic refusal to cite 'scientific' studies. Still, there are problems in the development of audience research in cultural studies. Most troubling is that we often hear too clearly the theorist's voice presented as if it were the audience's voice. This is especially true of cultural studies-based psychoanalytic accounts of audience activity, to which I would like now to turn briefly.

Psychoanalytic research in cultural studies

The literature in classical and contemporary psychoanalysis reveals the importance of analytical depth. Detailed information is gathered over a long period of time before therapeutic breakthroughs can be expected. The painstaking procedures of the psychoanalyst should be kept in mind, I believe, when we design or consider audience studies that promote psychoanalytic interpretations. Studies framed within the psychoanalytic tradition should meet the standards of psychoanalytic methodology. The subjectivity of this variety of research is not a problem; difficulties arise when we try to discern *whose* life is privileged in the analysis.

A cultural studies piece by Valerie Walkerdine (1986), for instance, exemplifies this problem. Walkerdine promotes a psychoanalytic/feminist position in a study she made of a family watching the video of the action film *Rocky II*. But in the text, Walkerdine included a childhood photograph of herself dressed as 'Tinky' (short for Disney's 'Tinkerbell'), a nickname her father gave her as a child which she now considers to be sexist and demeaning. Virtually the same event is then observed in her research. In her analysis of the family watching the video, a prominent theme is the meaning and importance of the father's nicknaming his little girl 'Dodo'. Walkerdine claims that the father's appreciation of violent imagery in the video is psychically related to his need to 'be a big man' and dominate his daughter by naming her with reference to an extinct, and therefore helpless, creature – the dodo bird.

What concerns me most about psychoanalytic research in general and this study in particular is sufficiency of evidence. Where does the evidence come from and how are explanations developed? Are the interpretive frames and specific details invoked in the analysis traceable to research subjects or do they actually represent the author more? If they represent the author, then the accounts should not be called 'cultural research'. What we have is autobiography. More productive approaches to psychoanalytic research would be for the writer to discuss the specifics of her own case, comment theoretically on hypothetical situations, or spend the time necessary to collect information that more authentically reveals the peculiarities and potential insights of other cases.

An example of an insightful psychoanalytic audience study, based on lengthy interactions with many families, is Jan-Uwe Rogge and Klaus Jensen's work in West Germany (Rogge and Jensen 1988). Relying on in-home observations and repeated depth interviews, these authors analyze the psychodynamics of families by employing what they term an 'empathic-interpretive method . . . that enters into the everyday worlds of families and seeks to understand [them] within the context of their individual and social frameworks' (p. 85). The authors develop many analytical themes regarding families' interactions with mass media by discussing the implications of telecommunications technology for individuals and for families as 'systems'. They support their inferences with observations and lengthy interview transcripts – concrete evidence that has been gathered over several years. We really come to know the families the authors have studied. While the stories of the families are told *through* and *by* the researchers, we never doubt that the psychoanalytic explanations provided by the researchers are grounded firmly in the life-worlds of the subjects.

Sufficiency of evidence: a (true) short story

As I write this piece I am in Acapulco, Mexico. It's 90 degrees Fahrenheit and sunny every day so (of course!) I must go to the beach. Among the groups of sunbathers stretched out in front of me today were four young Mexican women who were obviously friends. As I sat down, I noticed that these women were listening to an audio-cassette tape of American rock music by the Steve

Miller Band, the Grateful Dead, and Cat Stevens, on a high-quality sound system.

Intrigued by their use of American music, I casually analyzed the group. They were sunning themselves on a beach located directly in front of a luxury hotel. Okay, I thought, they're rich women from Mexico City. Upwardly mobile too. Expensive swim-suits and accessories, highbrow Castillian accent, American music – real jet-setters. (But the Steve Miller Band, the Grateful Dead, and Cat Stevens, for God's sake? Well, I figured, this is Mexico, not the United States. These recording artists mean something very different culturally here. As a researcher it is not my place to *evaluate* taste anyway.)

Let's put it all together: four young and obviously rich women have surrounded themselves with vivid symbols of upward mobility, the most revealing of which may be the public display of foreign-language music. Indeed, music may be the ultimate cultural validation of their aspirations; renouncing local culture, accepting the sound-track of an American lifestyle – quite a symbolic conversion in a culture so music-rich as Mexico. These women could in fact very well represent the world's new super class – an international economic elite – players in a post-modern environment comprised of layers of materialistic sophistication.

My theorizing collapsed moments later, however, when two gum-chewing female students from the University of Texas ('lady Long-horns') returned from a walk down the beach to reclaim their boom box and tapes from the Mexican women. 'Hey, thanks y'all for watchin' our stuff!' they said, picking up their equipment and music, returning to their beach towels nearby.

Let me use this brief example to make a distinction between details that comprise the *immediate context* and those that index the *referential context*. I was well on the way to constructing a (purposefully overblown for purposes here) cultural analysis of the Mexican women by carefully observing the immediate context. The details fit together well. Until the Americans returned, however, I did not have sufficient information about the referential context – how the details of any scene, no matter how meticulously observed and considered, fit within the larger context. And, of course, inter-viewing the subjects – letting them tell their own stories in their own words – would have provided indispensable additional evidence.

Analysis of any one act of media reception, no matter how cleverly interpreted, risks dramatic mistakes in interpretation. In fact, little ethnographic snapshots are even more error-prone than are the bits of information that can be retrieved about audience members through experimental or survey research. Identifying patterns of authentic human activity requires substantial immersion in its natural contexts, immediate and referential. The culminating critical incidents that often reveal so much about communication activity are meaningful and valid only when they are considered referentially.

External and internal validity

The most common criticism of qualitative empirical research coming from the social science quarter concerns the limits of its 'external validity' or 'representativeness'. Training in communication science has produced at least one generation of researchers who seem to be slaves to representativeness. In reality, of course, no truly random sample has ever been drawn and the use of convenience samples, usually college students or citizens of one community (college towns, normally), are commonplace in scientific research. Scientific researchers quietly compromise on the assumptions that underlie claims for external validity in their own work, yet 'insufficient generalizability' remains a favorite complaint made about qualitative empirical research.

For ethnographers, *internal* validity – the use of multiple streams of information converging *within* a particular study to construct an account of a complex investigatory theme – is far more important. Qualitative researchers typically focus on the subtleties and nuances of communication processes or the details of particular subgroups. The primary objective of qualitative empirical research, therefore, is not to assure that analytical accounts produced about certain families, peer groups, or subcultures can readily be generalized to other groups or settings (indeed, they often cannot be), but to explain well the phenomena, subjects, and contexts at hand. Our concern is with situated social action and theoretical representativeness, not with lawful behavior or statistical representativeness.

COMMUNICATION STUDIES AND CULTURAL STUDIES: COMPETITION OR COOPERATION?

Recognizing that substantial differences exist between communication studies (defined largely as it has been by the quantitative-scientific element) and cultural studies, I'm certainly not going to throw a party, invite everyone, and expect that all the contradictions

and conflicts will be ironed out. None the less, points of convergence and cooperation already exist. In fact, qualitative empirical
researchers in communication studies may have more in common
with cultural studies researchers than they do with quantitative
scientists. At the same time, many cultural studies researchers have
moved beyond the limits of strictly textual analysis to examine the
empirical life-worlds of audience members. A meeting ground may
have been found, therefore, between communication studies and
cultural studies in the practice of qualitative empirical research on
media audiences.

Furthermore, I believe that qualitative empiricism and the theoretical work that draws from it will have an increasingly important
impact on the development of communication and cultural theory
generally during the coming years. For many American researchers
trained in social science, cultural studies is the fresh breeze that we
have needed to feel (if we can just open the window!). Within
cultural studies, empirical analyses of media audiences became a
decidedly important (and controversial) development, especially in
the late 1980s. I consider my own work to be positioned somewhere
between communication studies and cultural studies. I am commit-
ted to rigorous empiricism (consistent with the methodological
ideals of science), but I have been impressed by the theoretical
visions of several cultural studies writers and believe that much of
this work is on the cutting edge of communication research.

The overlapping nature and integrative potential of qualitative
research in communication studies and cultural studies analyses of
media audiences, therefore, is indeed important and promising.
Researchers from both traditions, for instance, are interested in the
artistic artifacts and human interactions that comprise the construction of *popular* culture. This focus on popular media and audiences
is a powerful commonality in the academic environment where
studies of television texts and audiences are still considered by some
to be far less 'scholarly' than the study of classical literature, for
instance.

Both traditions also focus on *processes* of human communication.
These subtle and complex phenomena demand thematic and methodological diversity in research. Most cultural studies researchers,
for example, will continue to promote the importance of texts
and cultural contexts in media reception processes. Communication
studies researchers, meanwhile, are likely to concentrate more on
the social circumstances and activities of audiences and the flow of
information. Some researchers will count things, others will not.

It may also be possible, as Janice Radway (1988) has argued, to construct 'team ethnographies' with specialists concentrating on different areas. In fact, multimethodological designs of many types can be used, including quantification of certain types of information. In my study of family life with television in the People's Republic of China, for instance, several insights were gained by constructing simple statistical representations of things like family members' favorite genres of television programs, then relating that information to social and cultural issues (Lull 1988).

Furthermore, and most important, qualitative empirical research emanating from both communication studies and cultural studies can help to develop critical theory. Analysis of naturally occurring conversations, for example, can provide an underutilized means for seeing the subtle ways that ideology is woven into normative interaction by examining audience members' routine decoding practices. In general, ideological issues and the exercise of cultural power at the macro and micro levels can be addressed both by examining media texts and by looking concretely at audience interpretations and uses of media texts at times of reception and later.

Finally, qualitative empirical audience research can help us communicate with a wider public than is presently the case. By taking on fresh, relevant themes for analysis and writing accounts that play down methodological mystification and pretentious scientific or literary jargon, the new audience research may broaden its appeal both within the academy and outside it. Making our work interesting and useful to the public, it seems to me, should be a priority.

INTRODUCTION TO THE ARTICLES

The remaining chapters in this book are articles representing the major steps I have taken along a path of television audience research that has been developing during the last decade. The overall focus of the work is on the family as the 'natural' viewing group, but individual studies range from consideration of individuals within families to analyses of an entire society. My work is ethnographic. It relies primarily on direct observation and depth interviewing. Some of the empirical accounts combine statistical assessments with observations or interviews. In some cases, I collected all the data myself or with a co-researcher, while in other cases I trained students to gather the information. Particulars concerning methodology for each study are discussed in the individual chapters.

The foundation piece, 'The Social Uses of Television', best represents my early empirical and theoretical work. It is based on my doctoral research in Madison, Wisconsin, and subsequent field research that I carried out in Santa Barbara, California. From my very first studies of family television viewing, it was clear to me that people employ the medium extensively as a communication resource, not only during moments of viewing and not just at home. The emphasis in this article, therefore, is on the ethnomethodological features of television viewing, a microsocial-level analysis that situates television viewing within the normative contexts of everyday family life. The resulting typology of the social uses of television is reflected in much of my subsequent work.

In a companion piece published the same year, 'Family Communication Patterns and the Social Uses of Television', I tried to determine if families who differ in their characteristic styles of verbal interaction at home (social v. individualistic) also differ in the ways they use television. This was an attempt to link the social uses typology with a productive strain of family communication research ('family communication patterns') that emerged during the 1970s. This study reflects one of my past struggles – to make qualitative empirical research useful to the community of quantitative scientists in communication studies. The 'social uses' typology was therefore operationalized in the form of questionnaire items and correlational statistics were employed to assess relationships between items from the typology and family communication patterns.

Although my training was in communication science where, in America, the 'macro' issues are routinely ignored, I had been impressed by the analytical scope of political economic research ever since I read Herb Schiller's early books (Schiller 1969, 1973). I was searching for a way to link theoretically the microsocial communication processes I was studying with the macrosocial impacts that mass media unquestionably have. In Stuart Hall's theoretical development of the Gramscian concept of ideological hegemony, I could see how interpersonal communication stimulated by television content might be theorized critically and studied empirically. The fourth article in this volume, 'A Rules Approach to the Study of Television and Society', is a first step toward working out a critical perspective on my empirical work. Written more than ten years ago, the article promotes an explicit theoretical and implicit methodological turn away from mainstream communication research. Some of the formulations advanced in this piece now seem awkward to me, but a rules perspective continues to be a promising avenue for theorizing media audience activity.

The next piece, 'How Families Select Television Programs: A Mass-Observational Study', marks a return to the field to collect data relevant to the very first questions I had asked in developing my research on family involvement with television: Who chooses the shows at home and how is it done? This study synthesizes qualitative and quantitative methodological approaches and begins to demarcate family roles, based on family position, in terms of gender relations and family positions.

Certainly my most ambitious study is an ethnography of television audiences in the People's Republic of China, a research project that culminated in another book published by Routledge this year, *China Turned On: Television Reform, and Resistance*. The analysis is based on depth-interviews conducted with eighty-five families in Beijing, Shanghai, Guangzhou, and Xian and on discussions that were held with television programmers at the national network (CCTV) and the major regional stations. I have included here a section of the study that analyzes Chinese audience members' responses to the television serial *New Star*, a program that struck at the heart of China's internal problems and caused a tremendous national controversy. Many of the roots of the domestic unrest and violence that racked China in 1989 can be traced to problems that were addressed in this television series. This research project combines textual analysis with audience analysis, and shows how an ethnographic account can be developed to link family viewing practices with larger questions of politics, economics, and culture. The co-researcher referred to in the piece is Se-Wen Sun. I would like to point out that this draft was written before the student uprising and military repression in Beijing in the spring of 1989.

'Cultural Variation in Family Television Viewing' is a composite of two chapters from my edited international compilation of ethnographies, *World Families Watch Television*, published in 1988. The manuscript takes up theoretical issues that emerge from accounts written by scholars in England, Venezuela, West Germany, India, the United States, and the People's Republic of China as they each assess how television has been accommodated into everyday life routines in those nations. In this chapter I promote the idea that television viewing is an 'extension' – not only of the human senses, as McLuhan had argued, but of individual viewers, households, and cultures. In the end, I hope to show that families from all over the world watch television distinctively within their own cultures.

When I first began to do ethnographic research I was interested primarily in finding out how people choose and watch television programs at home and in analyzing the roles that television plays in family communication generally. But until I first observed and analyzed families in 1975, I was not sure that this type of audience research could be done successfully. Although I realized, for example, that television viewing is a fundamental family activity in the United States, I feared that families would depart from their routines in order to entertain me or to present a more favorable image of themselves. To any large degree, that simply did not happen. In reality, it is far too much work for families to maintain abnormal lifestyles for very long. This is one of the methodological issues that I take up in the last chapter, wherein I also discuss basic procedures for helping researchers learn how to get inside family viewing.

NOTES

1 Most of the Ivy League schools, including Harvard, Yale, and Princeton, and many other well-respected institutions that are based on the old model of disciplinary structuring, like the University of California at Berkeley, do not have departments of communication.

2 But while science makes a virtue out of being apolitical, its practitioners routinely work in, consult with, and are funded by government bureaucracies and major national and multinational corporations.

3 Even Hall's (1980a) introduction to work of the Birmingham center, cited here, was collectively proposed, discussed, and revised, according to the author.

4 A problem with the cultural studies' agenda, however, is that the work is so culturally insulated. So far we have seen very few accounts produced about cultures outside Great Britain, Europe, and North America.

5 And, in many cases, this was true.

6 Despite all the difficulties I encountered with the system as a whole, I will be forever grateful to my doctoral advisor at Wisconsin, Edwin Black. Professor Black was the first to help me see that ethnography is as close to rhetorical and literary studies as it is to social science. He encouraged my ethnographic research on audiences, work that at the time did not seem to fit well into established lines of empirical or critical research.

7 An American version of reception theory ('reader response') has been building during the past decade as well, an approach that is grounded in literary studies. See, for example, Fish (1979).

8 Two of the articles reprinted here were published originally by *Human Communication Research* during a far more inclusive and interesting period in the journal's history.

REFERENCES

Anderson, J. A. (1987) *Communication Research: Methods and Issues*, New York: McGraw-Hill.

Anderson, J. A. and Meyer, T. P. (1988) *Mediated Communication: A Social Action Perspective*, Newbury Park, CA: Sage Publications.

Ang, I. (1985) *Watching* Dallas: *Soap Opera and the Melodramatic Imagination*, London: Methuen.

_____ (1989) 'Wanted audiences: on the politics of empirical audience studies', in E. Seiter, H. Borchers, G. Kreutzner, and E. M. Worth (eds) *Remote Control: Television, Audiences, and Cultural Power*, London: Routledge.

Berger, C. R. and Chaffee, S. H. (eds) (1987) *Handbook of Communication Science*, Newbury Park, CA: Sage Publications.

Blumer, H. (1969) *Symbolic Interactionism*, Englewood Cliffs, NJ: Prentice-Hall.

Booth, C. (1970) *Life and Labor of the People of London*, New York: AMS Press.

Carey, J. (1985) 'Overcoming resistance to cultural studies', in M. Gurevitch and M. R. Levy (eds) *Mass Communication Yearbook 5*, Newbury Park, CA: Sage Publications.

Churchill, L. (1971) 'Ethnomethodology and measurement', *Social Forces* 50, 1: 4–13.

Dervin, G., Grossberg, L., O'Keefe, B. J., and Wartella, E. (eds) (1989) *Rethinking Communication*, Newbury Park, CA: Sage Publications.

Fish, S. (1979) *Is There a Text in This Class? The Authority of Interpretive Communities*, Cambridge, MA: Harvard University Press.

Gans, H. (1989) 'Sociology in America: the discipline and the public', *American Sociological Review* 54, 1: 1–16.

Garfinkel, H. (1967) *Studies in Ethnomethodology*, Englewood Cliffs, NJ: Prentice-Hall.

Glaser, B. G. and Strauss, A. L. (1967) *The Discovery of Grounded Theory: Strategies for Qualitative Research*, Chicago: Aldine.

Goffman, E. (1959) *The Presentation of Self in Everyday Life*, Garden City, NY: Doubleday.

_____ (1967) *Interaction Ritual: Essays on Face-to-Face Behavior*, Garden City, NY: Anchor Books.

_____ (1969) *Strategic Interaction*, Philadelphia: University of Pennsylvania Press.

Hall, S. (1979) 'Culture, the media, and the "ideological effect" ', in J. Curran, M. Gurevitch, and J. Woollacott (eds) *Mass Communication and Society*, Beverly Hills, CA: Sage Publications.

_____ (1980a) 'Cultural studies at the centre; some problematics and problems', in S. Hall, D. Hobson, A. Lowe, and P. Willis (eds) *Culture, Media, Language*, London: Hutchinson.

―――― (1980b) 'Encoding/decoding', in S. Hall, D. Hobson, A. Lowe, and P. Willis (eds) *Culture, Media, Language*, London: Hutchinson.

―――― (1986) 'The problem of ideology: Marxism without guarantees', *Journal of Communication Inquiry* 10, 2: 28–43.

Hamelink, C. (1983) 'Emancipation or domestication: toward a utopian science of communication', *Journal of Communication* 33, 3: 74–9.

Henry, J. (1965) *Pathways to Madness*, New York: Vintage Books.

Hymes, D. (1964) 'Introduction: toward ethnographies of communication', in J. J. Gumpertz and D. Hymes, *The Ethnography of Communication*, Menasha, WI; American Anthropological Association.

Jensen, K. B. (1986) *Making Sense of the News: Towards a Theory and an Empirical Model of Reception for the Study of Mass Communication*, Aarhus, Denmark: Aarhus University Press.

―――― (1987) 'Qualitative audience research: toward an integrative approach to reception', *Critical Studies in Mass Communication* 4, 1: 21–36.

―――― (1988) 'Answering the question: what is reception analysis?', *Nordicom Review of Nordic Mass Communication Research* 1: 3–5.

―――― (forthcoming) 'How to make a difference: communication theory, pragmatism, and mass media reception', in J. Anderson (ed.) *Communication Yearbook 14*, Newbury Park, CA: Sage Publications.

Kreiling, A. (1978) 'Toward a cultural studies' approach for the sociology of popular culture', *Communication Research* 5, 3: 240–63.

LaRossa, R. (1988) 'Renewing our faith in qualitative family research', *Journal of Contemporary Ethnography* 17, 3: 243–60.

LePlay, P. (1895) *L'Organisation de la famille selon le vrai modèle signale par l'histoire de toutes les races et de tous les temps*, Tours: A. Mame.

Lester, M. and Hadden, S. C. (1980) 'Ethnomethodology and grounded theory methodology', *Urban Life* 9, 1: 3–33.

Lewis, O. (1959) *Five Families*, New York: Basic Books.

―――― (1965) *La Vida*, New York: Random House.

Lindlof, T. (ed.) (1987) *Natural Audiences: Qualitative Research of Media Uses and Effects*, Norwood, NJ: Ablex.

Lull, J. (ed.) (1988) *World Families Watch Television*, Newbury Park, CA: Sage Publications.

Mehan, H. and Wood, H. (1975) *The Reality of Ethnomethodology*, New York: Wiley.

Morley, D. (1980a) 'Texts, readers, subjects', in S. Hall, D. Hobson, A. Lowe, and P. Willis (eds) *Culture, Media, Language*, London: Hutchinson.

―――― (1980b) *The 'Nationwide' Audience: Structure and Decoding*, London: British Film Institute.

―――― (1986) *Family Television: Cultural Power and Domestic Leisure*, London: Comedia.

Radway, J. (1984) *Reading the Romance: Feminism and the Representation of Women in Popular Culture*, Chapel Hill, NC: University of North Carolina Press.

_____ (1988) 'Reception study: ethnography and the problems of dispersed audiences and nomadic subjects', *Cultural Studies* 2, 3: 359–76.

Rogers, E. M. and Chaffee, S. H. (1983) 'Communication as an academic discipline', *Journal of Communication* 33, 3: 18–30.

Rogge, J.-U. and Jensen, K. (1988) 'Everyday life and television in West Germany: An empathetic-interpretive perspective on the family as system', in J. Lull (ed.) *World Families Watch Television*, Newbury Park, CA: Sage Publications.

Schiller, H. (1969) *Mass Communication and American Empire*, Boston: Beacon Press.

_____ (1973) *The Mind Managers*, Boston: Beacon Press.

Schramm, W. (1963) *The Science of Human Communication*, New York: Basic Books.

Stevenson, R. L. (1983) 'A critical look at critical analysis', *Journal of Communication* 33, 3: 262–69.

Thomas, W. I. and Znaniecki, F. (1918–20) *The Polish Peasant in Europe and America*, Boston: Gorham.

Walkerdine, V. (1986) 'Video replay: families, films and fantasy', in V. Burgin, J. Donald, and C. Kaplan (eds), *Formations of Fantasy*, London: Methuen.

Willis, P. (1980) 'Notes on method', in S. Hall, D. Hobson, A. Lowe, and P. Willis (eds) *Culture, Media, Language*, London: Hutchinson.

Zimmerman, D. (1978) 'Ethnomethodology', *American Sociologist* 13, 1: 6–15.

2 The social uses of television

Elihu Katz, director of the Hebrew University's Communication Institute, once told the British Broadcasting Corporation that he would give 'a large prize to anybody who succeeded in developing a method for the sampling of everyday conversation to supplement the probing of survey research' on mass communication (Katz 1977). He described the potential advantages of these data in the analysis of the media's role in setting conversational agendas, television's place in the development of interpersonal interaction patterns within families, the socialization effects of media, and the consequences of media programming on the use of language, patterns of speech, and thought.

The purpose of this essay is to elaborate theoretically and practically on Katz's recommendation for increased sensitivity by mass communication researchers to the nature of the social uses which audience members make of television. This will be accomplished by first suggesting that audience members create specific and sometimes elaborate practical actions involving the mass media in order to gratify particular needs in the social context of family television viewing. Second, a research method (ethnography) will be presented which allows for investigation of these media-related behaviors. Finally, evidence will be presented from ethnographic research in conjunction with pertinent findings from the uses and gratifications literature in support of a typology of the social uses of television.

MASS MEDIA AS SOCIAL RESOURCES

Social actors can be thought to employ actively the tools of communication in order purposively to construct their social realities. Symbolic interactionism (Blumer 1969), language-action (Frentz and

Farrell 1976), and communicative constructivism (Delia 1977) are, to varying degrees, contemporary derivatives of the social constructivist position. The uses and gratifications paradigm in mass communication is another manifestation of the constructivist view. Adherents to this perspective posit that individuals selectively use mass media in order to satisfy their human needs. In Katz' words, 'this is the research tradition which asks not what the media do to people, but what people do with the media' (Katz 1977). According to the modern conception, 'uses' of media are observable evidences of the audience's control over the content and receptive instruments of mass communication.

Less obvious social uses of television, many of which are embedded in the taken-for-granted communicative substance which surrounds the viewing experience, generally have not been examined. However, the recent tradition of ethnomethodology, wherein the assumptive world of social interaction is itself treated as a phenomenon (Garfinkel 1967; Mehan and Wood 1975; Zimmerman 1978; Zimmerman and Pollner 1970), provides a perspective to disclose additional insights into the nature of human communication, including interpersonal uses of the mass media.[1] Common social instances of media consumption can be viewed as delicate and situated accomplishments created by the persons involved.

In the study of human communication, specimens of language, occasions for talk, and the structural properties of interaction patterns can all be identified among available resources for the accomplishment of such interpersonal objectives as the creation of communicative displays which attest to the social competency of an interlocutor or to the correct fulfillment of role incumbencies (Hymes 1964; Philipsen 1975). These resources are so central to daily living that verbal strategies are even known to be utilized together with a host of other communicative provisions in order for a social member to display gender effectively (Garfinkel and Stoller 1967).

Mass media can also be viewed as important and uniquely employed social resources in interpersonal communication systems. They are handy expedients which can be exploited by individuals, coalitions, and family units to serve their personal needs, create practical relationships, and engage the social world. Television and other mass media, rarely mentioned as vital forces in the construction or maintenance of interpersonal relations, can now be seen to play central roles in the methods which families and other social units employ to interact normatively. The interpersonal uses one makes of the mass media constitute the construction of a particular subset of actions which find many practical applications in the home environment. One approach to documenting these behaviors is participant-observational research, which leads to ethnographies of mass communication.

THE ETHNOGRAPHIC METHOD IN THE STUDY OF MEDIA AUDIENCE BEHAVIOR

In mass communication research, the most fundamental aspects of human interaction – those distinct and detailed events which social actors create *in their own terms and on their own grounds* in order to make the substance of their ordinary routines meaningful – are seldom taken into account by researchers. The rough edges, special cases, and subtle peculiarities of the social world are sometimes ignored in order to facilitate cleanliness, parsimony, and predictive strength in mathematically induced designs and theories.

Participant observational strategies offer alternatives to the methods which are commonly employed. The use of participant observation for documentation of intensive naturalistic case studies in mass communication allows for theory building which binds together conceptual communicative elements, message linkages, and exchanges by social actors as holistic units-in-interaction (Blumer 1969). The family, television's primary audience, is a natural unit for this kind of analysis. Through ethnographic inquiry, the researcher can study actual communication contexts and ways in which media experiences enter the lives of family members.

A naturalistic research method which gains access to audience members' conversations alone, however, has not proven to be sufficient. This investigatory approach has been attempted with only moderate success by researchers from the Kansas City Mental Health Foundation (Bechtel *et al.* 1972). Television cameras were placed on top of the television sets of a small sample of families (twenty) in order to document viewing behavior. Microphones were placed around the room to record conversations and personal reactions to the shows. With this equipment, the researchers were able to observe behavior which accompanies television viewing (e.g. singing, ironing, sorting clothes, talking, mimicking the television, dancing, doing exercises, posing, dressing, fighting, eating). They also investigated the degree of agreement between the actual and estimated amounts of television viewing done by their subjects. A considerable discrepancy between the two measures was found, with significant overreporting of viewing time made by nearly half the family members.

By examining one distinct aspect of family life (the viewing experience), the researchers concluded that 'Television viewing does not occur in a vacuum; it is always to some degree background to a complex behavior pattern in the home. . . . No doubt an aim of future research is determining the relationships among viewing time, viewing styles, and the larger framework of a family's life style' (Bechtel *et al.* 1972: 299).

Bechtel and his associates concluded that even the most accurate record of movements and conversations in front of the set failed to provide much insight into the nature of interpersonal networks which characterize family communication systems. Further, the sampling of conversation alone did little to advance knowledge of the uses, gratifications, or meanings that media hold for their audiences. Patterns or styles of viewing were not regarded in relation to the substance of subjects' everyday interpersonal communications, their personality characteristics, family roles, or the structural properties of the families. Also, as one might suspect, viewing habits were reported by many subjects in this study to have been substantially altered by the presence of a vidicon camera pointing at them from the top of their television sets.

The more elaborate method of ethnography, which is organized around (1) participant observation, (2) the use of informants, and (3) in-depth interviewing, can be used by the social researcher as an integrated means for understanding the everyday world of social groups, their patterns of interpersonal communication, and their uses of the mass media. The intent of the ethnography of mass communication is to allow the researcher to grasp as completely as possible with minimal disturbance the 'native's perspective' on relevant communicative and sociocultural matters indigenous to him or her (Bruyn 1966; Glaser and Strauss 1967). The method, when applied to the study of television's primary audience, requires that the researcher enter the natural domain of his subjects – the family home. The willingness and abilities of the researcher are strongly tested by the prospect of this intrusion into such a small and private social unit.

The presence of the investigator in the habitat of his subjects, the usual objection to participant observation research, need not severely disrupt the natural behavior of the family unit (Lull 1976, 1978). Recently, I conducted some research on the ways in which families select television programs for group viewing in their homes

(Lull 1978). In order to collect these data, families were asked to gather in their homes when all members could be present. Family members were given six independent sets of fabricated program selections to choose from. Conversations were audiotape recorded as families decided what television shows to 'watch'. The nature of their overall discussion patterns, comparative willingness to express preferences, the degree of selection consensus, and perceptions of interpersonal influence in the family were later reported.

When I placed myself in the homes of families on these occasions, a variety of unexpected developments took place. I quickly became convinced that a more encompassing form of systematic, in-home participant observation could provide even more valuable insights into families' uses of the media. My arrival at subjects' residences during the study described above sometimes interrupted normal television viewing. In several cases, the negotiation of *real* choices for television viewing resumed before I had departed the home at the conclusion of the research exercise. I was greatly encouraged that, in this early study, where I had entered the homes of twenty families personally unknown to me, apparently normal television-viewing behavior took place with the researcher still present. Subsequent research, where observers spent from three to seven days with families, has demonstrated that, in the vast majority of cases (more than 80 percent), families indicated at the conclusion of the observational period that no major behavioral alterations had taken place due to the presence of the investigator.

When documenting the social uses of television by the ethnographic method, the researcher uses observations and interview data as a means for internal behavioral validation. Since multiple observer-coder strategies are impractical in most ethnographic research, the investigator combines detailed observations of the social unit with postobservational in-depth interviewing of the subjects. Further checks on the observed behaviors are made with the use of informants – in this case, other family members.

Three or four essential forms of raw data exist at the conclusion of the data-gathering process. Written materials include the observational notes made by the observer during the time spent in family homes. The observer also has produced a written summary at the end of each day of observation. Audio tape recordings have been made by interviewing each family member at the conclusion of the observational period. Written transcripts are made from the tape recordings.

A simple but useful technique has been to typewrite onto paper

or cards all the observational notes (including interview information) which will be used for compiling the ethnographic report.
Then, after a careful review of the data for themes to be explored
in the analysis, observations and interview comments are placed
together by cutting the typewritten pages into units or placing the
cards in the desired sequence. In this way the researcher can
arrange and rearrange the 'bits' of data until the proper internal
consistency is found within each topic. These data help the ethnographer of mass communication demonstrate the internal validity
of areas which are to be developed theoretically.

While participant observational strategies can be designed to test
specific hypotheses posited in advance of the period of observation,
this is typically done after an initial process of discovery has been
undertaken utilizing the same essential method (Cicourel 1974:
203).

The ethnography of mass communication is meant to be a sustained, microscopic, inductive examination of the natural interactional communications which connect human beings to the mass
media and to each other. From data generated by ethnographic
inquiries with this purpose, and by means of a review of the contributions made by other researchers to the uses and gratifications
literature, a beginning typology of the social uses of television has
been constructed and is presented in the next major section of this
chapter. Evidence presented in support of the typology derives from
a review of the major findings in the uses and gratifications literature
and from ethnographic data collected at the University of Wisconsin
and the University of California.

More than 200 families, representing blue-collar, white-collar,
and farm types, were studied during the past three years at these
locations. They were contacted through social agencies such as girls'
clubs, boys' clubs, community nursery schools, university resources,
and religious groups. In the variety of studies, families have been
randomly selected from mailing lists, telephone lists, or from members present at general meetings attended by the researcher. The
acceptance rate for families contacted was about 30 percent. This
figure is less when 'normal' families only (two parents present) are
used (Bechtel *et al.* 1972). Observational periods ranged from two
to seven days per family.[2] Observers studied these groups from
mid-afternoon until bedtime. Intensive independent interviewing of
each family member followed the last day of observation in each
case. Following the writing of the reports, family members were
asked to read and confirm the validity of the observations.

Families at first were given only a general introduction to the purpose of the research. They were told that the observers were students in communication who were interested in 'family life'. It was not possible to reveal the researchers' particular interests since that knowledge probably would have influenced families' media activities during the observational period. Debriefing followed the collection of all data.

Observers' procedures for data gathering were standardized as much as possible from family to family. Each observer maintained a preprinted log on which the ongoing behavior of families was documented throughout the day. Since they were known to the families only as students, the observers took most of their notes in the guise of 'homework' chores conducted while they sat in the living rooms or television-viewing areas of the homes. In this way, observers were able to take many notes on the premises and record the details of interpersonal interaction and media use as they occurred. A reconstruction of daily behavior was made by each observer after returning home following the observation period each night.

Observers took part in the routines of the families for the duration of the observation period. They ate with the families, performed household chores with them, played with the children, and took part in group entertainment, particularly television watching. Families were told from the beginning that in no case should they change their routines in order to accommodate the observer.

Observers looked for regularity in communicative acts reflected in the interpersonal roles and relationships associated with the use of mass media. Particular interactional behaviors such as dominance strategies and talk patterns were noted. Interpersonal behaviors involving mass media, such as the dynamics of the television program selection process and the viewing experience, were other primary areas for observation.

A full accounting of the data collected in studies such as this is not well suited for journal reports because of the lengthy analyses which typify ethnographic research. Family communication is so vivid, detailed, and theoretically intriguing under naturalistic conditions that the alert ethnographer becomes seemingly inundated by pertinent observations. Henry, in his accounts of five mentally disturbed families (Henry 1965), used about 100 pages of text to discuss each family. Lewis discussed the behavior of five Mexican families in 300 pages (Lewis 1959) and required nearly 700 pages to present a single Puerto Rican extended family (Lewis 1965).

Other classic ethnographies of neighborhoods, gangs, and cultures have also been reported in book-length form (Anderson 1923; Gans 1962; Liebow 1967; Whyte 1943). Ethnographic data presented in support of the following typology is, necessarily, a distillation of the findings.

THE SOCIAL USES TYPOLOGY

A previous attempt to organize audience uses of the mass media into a descriptive typology has been made by McQuail, Blumler, and Brown (1972). Their category system is arranged into four components: (1) diversion – the use of television and other media for escaping routines and problems, emotional release; (2) personal relationships – social utility, companionship; (3) personal identity – personal reference, reality exploration, value reinforcement; (4) surveillance.

In the following paragraphs, an accounting for the primary social uses, opposed to the personal uses implicit in much of the McQuail *et al.* schema, is presented. It is somewhat arbitrary to distinguish between the personal and interpersonal uses of television, however the inventory and explication of the uses of television described here focus directly on their communicative value as social resources.

Social uses of television in the home are of two primary types: structural and relational (Figure 2·1). The focus of this section will be on the latter category, but a brief discussion of the former is helpful in clarifying the different uses of the medium. Examples which illustrate components of the typology are by no means thought to be exhaustive of the individual categories. The evidence presented here is meant to provide an introductory agenda of behaviors which can be classified according to the factors which are described.

Structural uses of television

Television is employed as an *environmental resource* in order to create a flow of constant background noise which moves to the foreground when individuals or groups desire. It is a companion for accomplishing household chores and routines. It contributes to the overall social environment by rendering a constant and predictable assortment of sounds and pictures which instantly creates an apparently busy atmosphere. The activated television set guarantees its users a nonstop backdrop of verbal communication against which they can construct their interpersonal exchanges. Of course, it always serves its timeless environmental function as a source of entertainment for the family.

Figure 2.1 Social uses of television

Structural

Environmental: background noise; companionship; entertainment.

Regulative: punctuation of time and activity; talk patterns.

Relational

Communication facilitation: Experience illustration; common ground; conversational entrance; anxiety reduction; agenda for talk; value clarification.

Affiliation/avoidance: Physical, verbal contact/neglect; family solidarity; family relaxant; conflict reduction; relationship maintenance.

Social learning: Decision-making; behavior modeling; problem-solving; value transmission; legitimization; information dissemination; substitute schooling.

Competence/dominance: Role enactment; role reinforcement; substitute role portrayal; intellectual validation; authority exercise; gatekeeping; argument facilitation.

Second, television has the structural characteristic of being a *behavioral regulator*. Television punctuates time and family activity such as mealtime, bedtime, choretime, homework periods, and a host of related activities and duties. Patterns of talk are affected by viewing routines. External family communication is similarly regulated by television. Taking part in community projects, recreational activities, or outside entertainment are directly influenced by the scheduling of television programs.

Television viewing takes place in social units other than families. Viewing in various settings can be free and selective, as it is in college dormitories, or it can be parceled out as a reward granted by the proper authorities. Children in nursery schools are allowed to watch television after they pick up their toys. Girls in a California reform school can view only when their rooms pass inspection and when they complete their evening chores. Television in a retirement home is an attractive alternative to sitting alone in a private room. Under all these conditions, television viewing contributes to the structuring of the day. There is a time for viewing. That time is often related to other responsibilities and activities in which the individual is involved.

Relational uses of television

The ways in which audience members use television to create practical social arrangements can be organized into a behavioral typology of four major divisions. While the exclusivity of the categories is not absolute, an argument for the internal validity of the components of the schema described below will be made. Further, the order of presentation of the four relational functions (communication facilitation, affiliation/avoidance, social learning, competence/dominance) is made sequentially in order to demonstrate the relative complexity of the constructs.

Communication facilitation

Television's characters, stories, and themes are employed by viewers as abundant illustrators which facilitate conversations. Children, for example, use television programs and characters as primary known-in-common referents in order to clarify issues they discuss. Television examples are used by children to explain to each other, and to their parents and teachers, those real-world experiences, emotions, and beliefs which are difficult to make interpersonally transparent in attempts at verbal communication.

A child often uses television in order to enter an adult conversation. When a child is ignored during conversations held by adults, he or she can gain entry to the discussion by using a television example which illustrates a point being made by one of the adult interactants. If participants in the conversation are familiar with the television example, the child has introduced a common referent in order to gain access to the conversation from which he or she was otherwise left out.

The viewing experience itself can be facilitative. Conversational discomfort is sometimes reduced when the television is turned on and in view of the interactants. The uneasiness of prolonged eye contact is lessened since the television set ably attracts attention during lulls in conversation. Also, the program being watched creates an immediate agenda for talk where there may otherwise be none.

The medium is used as a convenient resource for entertaining outside guests in the home. To turn on the set when guests arrive is to introduce instant common ground. Strangers in the home may then indulge in 'television talk' – verbal responses to television programs which allow audience members to discuss topics of common experience which probably have little personal importance. Television viewing under these circumstances provides an opportunity for abundant talk with little substance – an exercise in conversational form for the interlocutors. In this way, viewers become better acquainted but invest minimal personal risk. Television also helps some family members clarify interpersonally their attitudes and values, especially in recent years since the medium has presented more controversial programming.

Affiliation/avoidance

A fundamental social use of television is its potential as a resource for the construction of desired opportunities for interpersonal contact or avoidance. One uses and gratifications researcher believes that this is the primary social use of the medium (Nordenstreng 1970). The proxemic nature of audience positioning in front of the television set is often used to advantage by young children who desire to engage physically or verbally their admired older siblings. Some adults orchestrate rare moments of physical contact in front of the television screen, an intimacy which need not be accompanied by conversation. An entertainment medium, however defined, is useful for this purpose. In one family which was observed, the husband and wife touched each other only twice during the seven-day period. The first time the man playfully grabbed his wife and seated her on his lap while his daughter, acting as a kind of medium, told a humorous story about something that had happened at school that day. The other occasion for physical contact during the week took place one night while the couple watched television. The man was a hard-working laborer who nearly always fell asleep when he watched television at night. He dozed as he sat in a recliner rocking chair with his shoes off. He snored loudly with his mouth open. His wife, who had been sitting on the floor in the same room, pushed herself along the floor until she was close to his chair. She learned back until her head rested against his bare feet and smiled as she created this rare moment of 'intimacy'.

Television viewing is a convenient family behavior which is accomplished *together*. The medium is used to provide opportunities for family members or friends to experience communal entertainment or informational programming. A feeling of family solidarity is sometimes achieved through television-induced laughter, sorrow, anger, or intellectual stimulation (Katz and Foulkes 1962). Confirmation of the family as a unit of interdependent personalities is made by the attempts of viewers to predict consensually the outcomes of television shows while they watch or by the creation of on-going discussions of the details or implications of the televised stories. Audience members also use television as a family relaxant whereby group viewing promotes family harmony by reducing interpersonal discord, at least during the viewing period.

Television can also *lessen* the demand for the manufacture of talk and the exchange of thought by providing a sustaining focus for attention which can be employed as a kind of social distractor, rendering less intense the communicative formalities which might otherwise be expected. Since television is used by the viewer as a focus for attention, creating 'parallel' rather than interactive viewing patterns, it also becomes a resource for escape – not just from the personal problems or responsibilities of the individual viewer, but from the social environment (Walters and Stone 1975). Anthropologist Edmund Carpenter (1972) reported that a US Army official in Germany recently blamed the high divorce rate among his troops on the lack of an English-language television station in the area where they live. The officer said, 'That means a soldier and his wife have got to talk to each other in the evenings and they suddenly discover that they really don't like each other' (Carpenter 1972: 10). A blue-collar family which was observed said it was grateful for television since it occupies so much of the grandparents' time in the evening, thereby keeping them away from their home which is located just three doors away. This young couple preferred not to be bothered by their parents. Television limits unwanted visits.

Television functions as a social resource in a unique way which helps married couples maintain satisfactory relationships. Unlike print media which transmit bits of information, television can provoke a vicarious, evanescent fantasy world which serves for some the psychological purpose of a desirable, if temporary, occupation of an alternative reality.

Psychological transformations triggered by program viewing become resources put to use by the inventive social actor. An example is revealed in the case of a farm woman who fifteen years ago resigned her pre-med scholarship to a major midwestern university, married her high-school boyfriend, and attended vocational school in order to become a medical secretary. Her first child was born one year following her marriage, causing her to quit her job at the medical office.

The *only* television shows watched by this woman during the research period were programs which featured settings and themes directly related to the medical profession ('Marcus Welby, MD', 'Medical Center', 'Medical Story'). When these programs were aired, she engaged in a continual and intense commentary about the nature of the story, particularly as it related to medical considerations. She remarked about the appropriateness of operating-room procedures. She evaluated the work of subordinates and always referred to the doctors by their formal titles. She praised medical work well done and found fault with mistakes made by the staff. The Caesarean section of quintuplets during one melodrama fascinated her as she remarked instructively about the importance of quickly trimming 'all five cords'.

During an interview probe following a week-long observation period conducted by the researcher, the woman said:

'I've always been interested in anything medical, in anything to do with the medical field. So, that's what I like . . . I usually find that their (medical) information is pretty accurate for their diagnosis of disease and so forth . . . so, I enjoy it because I worked around a lot of that and it just kinda keeps me in the business, I guess.'

Her husband appeared to recognize the desirability of using television as a fantasy stimulant for his wife. Although his wife knew full well what times her favorites were televised, he reminded her of these and encouraged her to watch. He even changed the television channel from 'Monday Night Football' in order to insure that she watched a medical program which was presented by a competing network at the same time. His encouragement of her participation in the dream world which their marriage and child raising denied her may have helped him dismiss whatever guilt he harbored for having been, in part, responsible for curtailing her vocational opportunities.

Social learning

Television is widely regarded as a resource for learning (Lyle 1972). Of special interest here are the social uses made of the many opportunities for learning from television. Much information for daily living is available from the electronic media. Obvious examples are the consumer and political spot messages which provide an agenda for decision-making, actions which have important implications for the society, the family unit, and the individual (Schiller 1973). But more subtle learning experiences have been noted as well. Early studies of the soap operas demonstrated that these melodramas provide practical suggestions for social interaction which are widely imitated by audience members (Herzog, 1944; Lazarsfeld and Stanton 1949). These imitations may be useful in the solving of family problems which bear resemblance to difficulties resolved in television dramas. At the very least, television provides an abundance of role models which audience members find socially useful.

Parents encourage their children to watch television game shows, public television, or network specials as substitute school experiences. Themes and values implicit in television programs are used by the parents to educate their children about the topics being presented in accord with their own views of the world. In this way, the value system of the parent is transmitted to the child and attitudes already in place are reinforced (Katzman 1972).

Scholarly research on how individuals learn from the mass media, then pass the information along in predictable interpersonal diffusion patterns, dates back more than thirty years (Berelson, Lazarsfeld, and McPhee 1954; Katz and Lazarsfeld 1962; Lazarsfeld, Berelson, and Gaudet 1948; Merton 1949). The two-step flow and the multistep flow theories implied that opinion leaders, who are heavy media consumers in their areas of expertise, learn much about their specialities from television and other media. These informational experts then transmit their knowledge to a network of human acquaintances.

In accomplishing the information-dissemination task, opinion leaders use information from the media to not only educate their friends, acquaintances, or co-workers, but also to assert themselves as valued members of society. The opinion leader uses television and other media to help create and then fulfill an interpersonal role which may have the effect of demonstrating competence.

Competence/dominance

There are a variety of ways in which television provides unique opportunities for the demonstration of competence by means of family role fulfillment. The regulation of children's television viewing by a parent is one means for accomplishing this objective. For those adults who desire to supervise closely or restrict the flow of unwanted external information into the home, the methodical and authoritative regulating of television viewing is useful as an occasion for the undertaking of a gatekeeping function. In doing so, the parent, often the mother, makes observable to the children and spouse a correct role-determined and rule-governed action which confirms the individual as a 'good parent' or 'good mother'. Successful enactment of the television regulatory function directs media experiences of the children into forms which are consistent with the parents' moral perspective. Simultaneously, the parent asserts an expected jurisdictional act which confirms proper performance of a particular family role.

The symbolic portrayal of roles by television characters may confirm similar roles which are undertaken by audience members. When behavior by an actor or actress on television resembles the way in which the viewer behaves under similar circumstances, the experience may be useful to the viewer as a means for demonstrating role competence to the other audience members. Similarly, a family member may use television in order to learn acceptable role behavior, then imitate this behavior in a way which results in acceptance of the role enactment by other family members.

The role of a missing parent can be played by a television character. It is convenient in some single-parent families for the adult who is present to encourage the watching of particular television programs where a favored image of the missing parent is regularly presented. Implicitly, the role of the lone parent can be preserved or clarified as the substitute parent's complementary actions are portrayed on the screen.

Some viewers capitalize on the one-way nature of television by verbally assaulting the characters, newscasters, or commercials. One man who was observed constantly disagreed out loud with the evening news reports on television. He clarified the reports and chided the announcer for not knowing the 'real facts'. Vocal criticisms of programs or commercial announcements also serve as ways for viewers to reassure one another that, despite the fact that they are now watching, they know how *bad* television is, a self-promoting evaluation.

In another case, a housewife who majored in French in college repeatedly corrected the poor pronunciation of French words uttered by an American actor who attempted to masquerade as a Frenchman. Gans, in a study of poor Italian families in Boston, found that his subjects received attention from other viewers when they noticed that activities on the screen were technically unfeasible or when they pointed out 'anachronisms or mistakes [that] appear in the plot' (Gans 1962: 194).

A television viewer may or may not use the medium to demonstrate competence for purposes of dominating other family members. But cases in which this occurs are numerous in ethnographic research. For instance, family members often use television as a validator of contested information, thereby demonstrating intellectual competence. In one family, for example, the capture and arrest of William and Emily Harris of the Symbionese Liberation Army was a topic of conversation at the dinner table on the evening the couple was apprehended in San Francisco. There were conflicting reports among family members as to whether or not Patty Hearst had also been captured. The highly authoritarian father had heared an early report on radio that only the Harrises had been arrested. He had not learned the later news that Hearst had been taken into the custody of police as well. His wife and daughter *both* told him that they had heard on the car radio that Hearst had been arrested too. He arrogantly denied the validity of their reports and said that the family could find out the 'true situation' by watching the news of television. The husband later was embarrassed to discover on the news that Hearst had indeed been apprehended, a turn of events which falsified his version of the incident. 'See,' his wife said emphatically when the news was revealed. 'We were right! I told you that Patty Hearst had been caught and you wouldn't believe me.' The medium had confirmed her and disconfirmed him on the issue. A few minutes later television provided an opportunity for him to recapture his dominant position. During a commercial message, he voiced an opinion about some attribute of the product which was being promoted. His wife disagreed. Seconds later the television announcer on the commercial gave information which supported the husband. He quickly and defiantly turned to his wife and said, 'I don't talk much. But when I do you should listen.'

Men, women, boys, and girls use television to communicate to each other attitudes toward the appropriateness of male and female behavior with respect to sex roles. Teenaged boys were observed shouting criticism at the female detectives on the program 'Charlie's Angels' with their sisters in the room. The program provided an opportunity for the boys to vocalize their negative feelings about the qualifications of the television actresses for doing 'men's work'. Similarly, adolescent girls competed to correctly identify wardrobe fashions of various historical periods during a program which featured this topic. The girls tried to identify the periods before the announcer on the program did so. Correct identification gave status to the girl who guessed right, validating her as a relative expert on women's fashions and placing her in an esteemed position in the eyes of her peers.

Interpersonal dominance strategies involve television in other ways. Television viewing in many homes is authoritatively granted or taken away as a reward or punishment. Adults and children argue to decide who will watch what programs, thereby creating an opportunity for the airing of personal differences. For family members who are angered by each other, television viewing (the program decision-making process or the viewing experience) provides incessant opportunities for argument, provoking possible dominance struggles among family members.

More subtle uses of the medium are made by some viewers to influence other audience members. In one case, a married couple watched a television program in which the lead actor passionately embraced a young woman. The husband at home asked his wife during the scene if the two on the screen were married. She answered, 'Do they look married to you?' They both laughed quietly without taking their eyes off the screen. By co-orienting and commenting on the television program, these family members spoke to each other indirectly, but made their positions about relational matters clearly known.

CONCLUSIONS

Although the natural television audience, the family, has been identified in social theorizing as a 'unit of interacting personalities' since the work of Burgess (1926), the study of various family processes as they occur at home has seldom been tried. Further, researchers who study family behavior today have recognized that 'communication is increasingly emphasized as both the keystone of family interaction and the key to understanding family dynamics' (Anderson and Carter 1974: 111). Hopefully, this chapter has helped demonstrate that the methods which individuals construct, using television and other media, constitute important subsets of unique and useful communicative behaviors which are central to family life.

The typology of social uses of television presented here is different from previous ones in that the categories were derived by examining accumulated instances of observed audience behavior, detailed reports from audience members whose confidence had been won due to prolonged contact with field researchers, discussions by these same family members about the television uses employed by their peers, and by the relevant findings produced by other researchers using traditional data-gathering techniques. The contribution made to this work by the ethnographic method complements the data rendered by quantitative techniques and perhaps discloses some insights not otherwise obtainable. Knowledge of audience behavior in the family home can perhaps be maximized with a multi-method approach to this general area of inquiry, wherein data retrieved by traditional methods is considered in conjunction with ethnographic data.

While the typology of social uses presented here implies no particular ordering of the constructs other than by their apparent relative complexity, they can be considered ordinal and interdependent. As has been discussed, the social learning process on some occasions necessarily precedes the demonstration of role competence. Similarly, demonstration of role competence may take the more elaborate form of an interpersonal dominance strategy. Interpersonal affiliation may also be regarded as a precursive behavior with competence demonstration or domination as intended consequences of the move toward another family member. Communication facilitation seems intuitively fundamental to the three other categories.

It may be very helpful to construct indices based on the four major divisions of the relational uses of television to develop 'viewer types' or 'family types'. In doing so, it may be possible to determine if a person or a particular family uses television essentially for the facilitation of effective family communication; for the potential to construct the desired degree of interpersonal affiliation; for learning about how to behave in the social world; or for demonstrating competence or dominating others in the viewer group. Distinguishing these family types would generate an index of audience behavior as an independent variable. From this, researchers could design studies which would employ 'social uses types' as predictors of media exposure, interpersonal communication satisfaction, family harmony, or other relevant dependent measures of theoretical value. Audience behavior may then contribute more significantly to the growing interest in styles and strategies of family communication. The relational uses which families make of television certainly represent a range of communicative behaviors which reveal much about the nature of the group. A precise understanding of the particular uses made of television by families may even hold implications for family therapy.

Typologies are inherently descriptive and heuristic devices. The classification of social uses which has been presented here requires further elaboration and validation. Methodologically, an argument has been made for more ethnographies of mass communication, using triangulated data-collection techniques: naturalistic observation, self-reports, and other-reports. In this way, novel and complex social uses of television and other media can be documented. Another approach would be to operationalize the constructs proposed in the previous discussion in the form of fixed-alternative statements for survey research. By generating quantitative scores and applying statistical tests, it may be possible to establish or modify the components of the typology into scientifically intercorrelated factors. Of course, this method assumes that audience members are sufficiently self-aware to recognize or gauge some rather subtle uses of the media which have been discovered ethnographically, an assumption which may not be comfortably met.

This chapter was originally published in *Human Communication Research*, 4, 3, 1980.

NOTES

1 Ethnomethodology is, in a general sense, a manner for conducting social research since it is a way of thinking about social structure and process. But the term is intended to direct researchers to observation and interpretation of the social 'methods' of their subjects as the substance for analysis, particularly routine behaviors which are often overlooked. The 'method' in 'ethnomethodology' refers to the ways in which people construct their social realities, not to a research strategy.

2 For family research, a one-week-long observation period per family is most efficient. Henry (1965: xv-xxiii) makes a convincing argument for this length of observation. Certainly some additional data would be gathered in a longer stay, but the researcher must utilize the time wisely in order to maximize sample size while simultaneously retrieving the most valuable date.

REFERENCES

Anderson, N. (1923) *The Hobo*, Chicago: University of Chicago Press.

Anderson, R. E. and Carter, I. E. (1974) *Human Behavior in the Social World*, Chicago: Aldine.

Bechtel, R., Achelpohl, C., and Akers, R. (1972) 'Correlates between observed behavior and questionnaire responses on television viewing', in E. A. Rubinstein, G. A. Comstock, and J. P. Murray (eds) *Television and Social Behavior, 4: Television in Day-to-Day Life*, Washington, D.C.: United States Government Printing Office.

Berelson, B., Lazarsfeld, P., and McPhee, W. N. (1954) *Voting: A Study of Opinion Formation in a Presidential Campaign*, Chicago: University of Chicago Press.

Blumer, H. (1969) *Symbolic Interactionism*, Englewood Cliffs, NJ: Prentice-Hall.

Bruyn, S. (1966) *The Human Perspective in Sociology: The Method of Participant Observation*, Englewood Cliffs, NJ: Prentice-Hall.

Burgess, E. W. (1926) 'The family as a unit of interacting personalities', *The Family* 1, 1: 3–9.

Carpenter, E. (1972) *Oh! What a Blow that Phantom Gave Me*, New York: Holt, Rinehart & Winston.

Cicourel, A. (1974) *Theory and Method in a Study of Argentine Fertility*, New York: Wiley.

Delia, J. G. (1977) 'Constructivism and the study of human communication', *Quarterly Journal of Speech* 62, 1: 66–83.

Frentz, T. S. and Farrell, T. B. (1974) 'Language-action: a paradigm for communication', *Quarterly Journal of Speech* 62, 4: 333–49.

Gans, H. (1962) *The Urban Villagers*, New York: Free Press.

Garfinkel, H. (1967) *Studies in Ethnomethodology*, Englewood Cliffs, NJ: Prentice-Hall.

—— and Stoller, R. J. (1967) 'Passing and the managed achievement of sex status in an "intersexed" person. Part 1', in H. Garfinkel, *Studies in Ethnomethodology*, Englewood Cliffs, NJ: Prentice-Hall.

Glaser, B. G. and Strauss, A. L. (1967) *The Discovery of Grounded Theory: Strategies for Qualitative Research*, Chicago: Aldine.

Henry, J. (1965) *Pathways to Madness*, New York: Vintage Books.

Herzog, H. (1944) 'What do we really know about daytime serial listeners?', in P. Lazarsfeld and F. N. Stanton (eds) *Radio Research: 1942–43*, New York: Duell, Sloan & Pearce.

Hymes, D. (1964) 'Toward ethnographies of communication', *American Anthropologist* 66, 6: 1–34.

Katz, E. (1957) 'The two-step flow of communication: an up-to-date report on an hypothesis', *Public Opinion Quarterly* 21, 1: 61–78.

—— (1977) 'Looking for trouble: social research on broadcasting', lecture given to the British Broadcasting Corporation, London.

—— and Foulkes, D. (1962) 'On the use of mass media as "escape" ', *Public Opinion Quarterly* 26, 4: 377–88.

—— and Lazarsfeld, P. (1962) *Personal Influence: The Part Played by People in the Flow of Mass Communication*, Glencoe, Ill.: Free Press.

Katzman, N. (1972) 'Television soap operas: what's been going on anyway?' *Public Opinion Quarterly* 36, 2: 200–12.

Lazarsfeld, P., Berelson, B., and Gaudet, H. (1948) *The People's Choice*, New York: Columbia University Press.

—— and Stanton, F. N. (eds) (1949) *Communications Research: 1948–1949*, New York: Harper.

48   *Inside Family Viewing*

Lewis, O. (1959) *Five Families*, New York: Basic Books.
_____ (1965) *La Vida*, New York: Random House.
Liebow, E. (1967) *Talley's Corner*, New York: Little, Brown & Co.
Lull, J. (1976) 'Mass media and family communication. An ethnography of audience behavior'. Doctoral dissertation, University of Wisconsin-Madison.
_____ (1978) 'Choosing television programs by family vote', *Communication Quarterly* 26, 1: 53–7.
Lyle, J. (1972) 'Learning from television', in E. A. Rubenstein, G. A. Comstock, and J. P. Murray (eds) *Television and Social Behavior, 4: Television in Day-to-Day Life*, Washington, D.C.: United States Government Printing Office.
McQuail, D., Blumler, J. G., and Brown, J. R. (1972) 'The television audience: a revised perspective', in D. McQuail (ed.) *Sociology of Mass Communication*, Harmondsworth, England: Penguin Books.
Mehan, H. and Wood, H. (1975) *The Reality of Ethnomethodology*, New York: Wiley.
Merton, R. K. (1949) 'Patterns of influence', in P. Lazarsfeld and F. Stanton (eds) *Communications Research: 1948–1949*, New York: Harper.
Nordenstreng, K. (1970) 'Comments on "gratification research" in broadcasting', *Public Opinion Quarterly* 34, 2: 130–2.
Philipsen, G. F. (1975) 'Speaking like a man in teamsterville: culture patterns of role enactment in an urban neighborhood', *Quarterly Journal of Speech* 61, 1: 13–22.
Schiller, H. I. (1973) *The Mind Managers*, Boston: Beacon Press.
Walters, J. K. and Stone, V. A. (1975) 'Television and family communication', *Journal of Broadcasting*: 19, 4: 409–14.
Whyte, W. F. (1943) *Street Corner Society*, Chicago: University of Chicago Press.
Zimmerman, D. H. (1978) 'Ethnomethodology', *The American Sociologist* 14, 1: 6–15.
_____ and Pollner, M. (1970) 'The everyday world as a phenomenon', in J. D. Douglas (ed.) *Understanding Everyday Life*, Chicago: Aldine.

3 Family communication patterns and the social uses of television

When television researchers probe theoretical issues involving audience behavior, they often implicitly study families, the most pervasive viewing group. The social realities which audience members face at home contribute greatly to the varying 'uses' which individuals make of the mass media (Adoni 1979; Blumler 1979; Blumler and Katz 1974; Katz *et al.* 1974; McQuail *et al.* 1972; Nordenstreng, 1970; Swanson 1979). Television programs do not simply *arrive* uniformly in the homes of their audiences. Programs and commercials are received, interpreted, and acted upon in many different ways by individuals and families.

Empirical research has demonstrated that one factor which influences the way families process television is the nature of interpersonal communication which takes place at home. The major investigations which have been conducted on this topic are survey studies undertaken by Chaffee, McLeod and their associates at the University of Wisconsin-Madison (Chaffee *et al.* 1966, 1971, 1973; McLeod *et al.* 1967, 1972; Ward 1968). From this research, an identification of family types, based upon differential characteristics of parent–child verbal interaction, has emerged.

The essential construct which underlies the work of these researchers is a family communication patterns typology. Families are conceptualized on a two-dimensional basis. According to the model, parents emphasize some combination of 'structural relations' in raising their children (Chaffee *et al.* 1973). The dimensions have been termed 'socio orientation' and 'concept orientation'.

In socio-oriented families, parents strongly encourage their children to get along well with other family members and friends. The child is advised to give in on arguments, avoid controversy, repress anger, and stay away from trouble in general. Concept-oriented families, on the other hand, create a communicative environment where parents stimulate their children to express ideas and challenge others' beliefs. The child is exposed to more than just one side of a controversial issue and is encouraged to discuss or debate controversies with adults. In general, the difference between the family types is a preoccupation with others' feelings (socio) compared to an emphasis on presenting and discussing ideas (concept). These two communicative orientations have proven uncorrelated in a variety of populations (Chaffee *et al.* 1973).

The style of family communication contributes to the child's 'cognitive mapping' of situations encountered outside the family context (Chaffee *et al.* 1966). These socializing influences persist into adulthood and become part of the individual's personality inside and outside the home (McLeod *et al.* 1967). Patterns of family communication also contribute to the processes of political socialization. Concept-oriented families stimulate children to a higher level of political participation than is characteristic of socio-oriented families (Chaffee *et al.* 1973).

In conversations, socio-oriented individuals are more agreeable, supportive, and self-disparaging, while concept-oriented persons ask for and give more facts and opinions and frequently disagree with their interlocutors (Ward 1968). Concept-oriented children make better grades in school (while spending less time with homework), are more active in school, and want to be more like their parents than children from socio-oriented communication backgrounds (Chaffee *et al.* 1966). Socio orientation correlates positively with all forms of parental control, verbal and restrictive punishment, and with affection (McLeod *et al.* 1972). Concept orientation also correlates positively with affection (McLeod *et al.* 1972). Socioeconomic status is related to both socio-oriented families and concept-oriented families, but in different directions: -0.25 with socio orientation and $+0.41$ with concept orientation (McLeod *et al.* 1972). These studies, when taken together, rather clearly define some differences in attitudes and activities characteristic of family members who represent the two types of communication patterns.

Family members with socio and concept orientations also differ in their uses of the mass media. Parents and children in socio-oriented families have high levels of total television viewing, but are low in news consumption for all media (Chaffee *et al.* 1971; McLeod *et al.* 1972). Children from socio orientations are also quite high in viewing violent television (McLeod *et al.* 1972) and parent–child modeling for entertainment and news programs on television was demonstrated for socio families only (Chaffee *et al.* 1971).

Concept-oriented children use the mass media primarily for news and comparatively little for 'escape' entertainment (Chaffee *et al.* 1971). Concept-oriented family members have relatively low television consumption overall, exercise considerable control over television, and interpret television violence (McLeod *et al.* 1972). Adolescents from these families are not likely to identify with violent characters on television, nor are they likely to link television characters to real life (McLeod *et al.* 1972).

The purpose of the present research was to examine the relationship between family members' perceptions of the communication environment in their homes and the ways in which these individuals say they use television for the accomplishment of interpersonal objectives in the family context. The unit of analysis was the individual family member, not the family unit, since the research was conducted from a perspective that regards the individual as participating in strategic patterns of interaction which involve the employment of media as personal resources for accomplishing social tasks. The research was designed to determine if family members who hold differing perceptions of the nature of the communication environment at home also differ in the ways in which they use television socially.

An elaborate inventory of the social uses of television has recently been presented (Lull 1980). In that study, a typology of the social uses of the medium was generated following an ethnographic investigation of more than 200 families representing blue-collar, white-collar, and farm types. Television was found to be useful to family members for purposes which range from structuring daily activities and talk patterns to far more subtle and involved tasks such as conflict reduction, the reinforcement of family roles, and intellectual validation as a means for dominating another family member.

More than thirty individual uses of television were documented and categorized into a six-part typology which acknowledged a primary division between structural and relational uses of the medium. Structural uses are *environmental* (background noise, companionship, entertainment) and *regulative* (punctuation of time and activity, talk patterns). Relational uses of television include *communication facilitation* (experience illustration, common ground, conversational entrance, anxiety reduction, agenda for talk, value clarification); *affiliation/avoidance* (physical, verbal contact/neglect, family solidarity, family relaxant, conflict reduction, relationship maintenance); *social learning* (decision-making, behavior modeling, problem-solving, value transmission, legitimization, information dissemination, substitute schooling); and *competence/dominance* (role enactment, role reinforcement, substitute role portrayal, intellectual validation, authority exercise, gatekeeping, argument facilitation).

Most of the individual components of the social uses of television listed above were operationalized as questionnaire items for use in this correlational study. In order to achieve the objectives of this research, subjects' responses to these items were examined in relation to survey items which inquired of their family communication patterns.

METHOD

Subjects

Ninety-seven families comprising nearly 400 individuals were originally included in a quota sample which was drawn from members of the Girls' Club in Goleta, a Southern California community of about 70,000. These families agreed to let an observer-interviewer spend three days with them, the first two days observing and the final day interviewing family members. Because of illnesses, the arrival of unexpected guests, or sudden changes of mind, the number of families which took part in the research was 85, involving 352 individuals. Children who were less than 7 years old, and therefore unable to respond to the postobservational fixed-item questionnaire with validity, were eliminated from the subject group, thereby reducing the overall sample size to 327. Some 66 of the 85 families were two-parent groups. In the remaining 19 families, only 1 parent lived at home with the children, usually the mother. Some 82 mothers, 68 fathers, and 179 children were interviewed.

Survey items

Three conceptual areas were probed by means of the interview schedule. These areas were (1) family communication patterns, (2) the social uses of television, and (3) estimated amount of television viewing.

For family communication patterns, the questionnaire items which were used to measure the degree of each person's concept orientation and socio orientation were the same indices employed by Chaffee *et al.* during the past several years. Items which measured the concept orientation were:

(1) How often do you talk at home about things like politics or

religion where one person takes a different side from the others?

(2) How often do you (your parents) say that getting ideas across is important even if others don't like it?

(3) How often do you (your parents) encourage other family members to challenge each other's ideas and beliefs?

The socio orientation items were:

(1) How often do you (your parents) say that children should give in on arguments rather than make people angry?

(2) How often do you (your parents) say that children shouldn't show anger in discussions?

(3) How often do you (your parents) say that children shouldn't argue with adults?

All survey items within the same theoretical category (concept orientation, socio orientation) correlated highly with each other ($p < 0.001$ for each concept orientation item with every other concept item; $p < 0.001$ for each socio orientation item with every other socio item). Further, concept items were uncorrelated with socio items ($r = 0.01$, $p < 0.42$).

Data-gathering procedures

Trained observers (upper-division, undergraduate communication students) lived with the families from mid-afternoon until bedtime for two consecutive days, November 14–15 (Tuesday and Wednesday), 1978. The interviews were conducted on the following day. The data which pertain to this study were gathered during the interview session. The fact that an observational period preceded the interviewing has importance for this study. Interviewing which follows lengthy observation is much different from telephone or doorstep surveys where the researcher is not known by the subjects. The researcher is generally able to establish a high degree of rapport with his or her subjects during time spent in their homes. This provides an opportunity for friendly and productive postobservational interviewing. An unusual degree of trust is likely to lead to willingness on the part of the subjects to answer the questions carefully and with validity. This is especially advantageous when the questions are of a sensitive nature.

FINDINGS

The results of this study are reported below in two ways. First, each social use item is considered in terms of its value to the subjects without consideration of their family communication patterns. These values can be learned by examining the mean scores generated for each item (Table 3.1). By comparing these scores with each other, it is possible to find out which of the social uses of television are reported to be employed frequently by family members. A four-point Likert-type scale was used during the interviews which ranged from strongly agree (4) to strongly disagree (1). Therefore, any score greater than 2.5 indicates that the subjects as a group agreed that the social use item was employed by them.

With this criterion for evaluation, several items emerged as useful to the subjects. The use of television selectively to regulate the experiences of children (gatekeeping function) was the highest rated. Other highly rated items were the use of television for family

Table 3.1 Correlations of social uses of television with family communication patterns

Social use	Scores	Family communication type Socio orientation	Concept orientation
Environmental			
Background noise	1.8	0.20**	0.06
Companionship	2.7	0.24**	−0.16**
Entertainment	3.0	0.09*	0.00
Regulative			
Punctuate time	2.1	0.22**	−0.08
Talk patterns	2.5	0.16**	0.13**
Plan activities	1.8	0.21**	−0.10
Communication facilitation			
Experience illustration	2.1	0.30**	−0.13**
Common ground	2.3	0.19**	−0.05
Conversational entrance		0.28**	−0.30**
(children only)	2.2		
Anxiety reduction	1.9	0.22**	−0.20**
Agenda for talk	2.5	0.27**	−0.13**
Affiliation/avoidance			
Verbal contact	1.9	0.19**	−0.08
Family solidarity	2.4	0.12*	−0.02
Family relaxant	3.0	0.18**	−0.04
Conflict reduction	1.6	0.27**	−0.07

Social learning

Decision-making (consumer)	2.3	0.13**	−0.21**
Behavior modeling	1.8	0.29**	−0.11*
Problem-solving	1.7	0.21**	−0.04
Value transmission (parents only)	2.0	−0.16**	0.29**
Information dissemination	2.6	0.05	0.03
Substitute schooling	2.0	0.06	−0.04
Competence/dominance			
Role reinforcement	2.3	0.23**	−0.11*
Substitute role portrayal (single parents only)	1.8	−0.11*	−0.07
Intellectual validation	2.4	0.26**	0.05
Authority exercise (parents only)	2.2	−0.12*	0.29**
Gatekeeping (parents only)	3.4	−0.16**	0.31**
Argument facilitation	2.0	0.21**	0.10*

Note: Entries are Pearson product-moment zero-order correlations. A positive or negative correlation of 0.09 was required to reach significance at p <0.05 (*); a ±0.13 correlation or beyond was significant at p <0.01 (**).

entertainment, as a family relaxant, for companionship, for information dissemination, as an agenda for talk, and as a regulator of talk patterns which accompany viewing. Other items which were rated relatively highly were: to establish common ground, for consumer decision-making, for conversational entrance, for verbal contact, as a role reinforcer, for intellectual validation, and as a resource for exercising authority.

The data which are of central interest here, however, pertain to the relationship between differential communication patterns and the social uses of television. The second and third columns of figures in Table 3.1 are summed socio and concept measures correlated with scores which reflect subjects' reported degree of use of television for the various purposes indicated. As shown, socio- and concept-oriented individuals differed significantly in their reported social uses of television. In general, socio-oriented individuals were far more likely than concept-oriented persons to report that they employ television for social purposes. Correlations between measures of socio orientation and the social uses of television were, in most cases, significant in the positive direction. Correlations between concept orientation measures and the social uses indices were generally negative. Most of the correlations differed significantly from zero, indicating that statistical differences, for nearly all the items, were found between socio- and concept-oriented subjects.

In order to provide a framework for discussion, the uses of television by socio-oriented subjects will be reported next, followed by a description of the findings in relation to concept-oriented respondents.

Socio-oriented family members

Consistent significant, positive correlations were found between the socio orientation indices and measures of the social uses of television. Socio-oriented individuals use television for creating background noise, for companionship, to punctuate time, to regulate talk and plan activities, to illustrate experience, to provide common ground, for conversational entrance, to reduce anxiety, to provide an agenda for talk, for verbal contact, as a family relaxant, to reduce conflict in the home, to model behavior, to solve problems, to make consumer decisions, to reinforce roles, for intellectual validation, and to facilitate arguments ($p<0.01$). The medium was also regarded as useful for entertainment and to demonstrate family solidarity ($p<0.05$).

There were some significant negative correlations between the socio indices and the social uses of television. For instance, socio-oriented parents indicated that television was not used by them in order to regulate the experiences of their children through a gatekeeping activity or to transmit values to their children ($p<0.01$). Further, television was not useful for exercising authority, or for providing substitute role portrayals in single-parent families ($p<0.05$).

Concept-oriented family members

The correlations between summed concept orientation items and the social uses of television indices were generally negative and low. Individuals who had high cumulative scores on the concept-orientation measures said they did *not* use television for companionship, to illustrate experiences, to give them something to say, to reduce interpersonal anxiety, to make consumer decisions, or to gain conversational entrance ($p<0.01$). They also reported that they did not use the medium in order to plan their activities, to model their behavior, or as a role reinforcer ($p<0.05$).

There were some positive correlations between the concept orientation measures and the social uses of television. Parents who scored high on the concept indices indicated that they use the medium as a means to transmit values to their children, to regulate their children's behavior via gatekeeping, and to provide opportunities for the exercise of authority at home ($p<0.01$). High concept-oriented respondents also rated television as useful for the facilitation of arguments and as a regulator of talk patterns ($p<0.05$).

Television exposure and family communication patterns

The amount of television viewing done by subjects in this study correlated positively with socio orientation scores, particularly for fathers and mothers (Table 3.2). The amount of viewing was uncorrelated with concept orientation scores except for children aged 12–15, where a significant negative correlation was found. Young children were the heaviest viewers of television overall.

Table 3.2 Correlations of amount of television viewing with family communication pattern measures by family members

Person	Estimated television hours (weekly)	Summed concept–orientation scores[1]	Summed socio–orientation scores
Father ($n = 68$)	12.7	−0.10	0.45**
Mother ($n = 82$)	13.4	−0.08	0.26**
Children 16+ ($n = 41$)	11.4	0.15	0.16
Children 12–15 ($n = 62$)	16.8	−0.23*	0.08
Children 7–11 ($n = 76$)	15.7	0.07	0.16

1. Summed concept and socio scores are Pearson product moment zero-order correlations.
$N = 329$
**$p<0.01$
*$p<0.05$

DISCUSSION

This research was designed to determine if individuals from families which stress harmonious social relations differ in the ways they use television socially from family members who say they live in homes where the independent expression of ideas characterizes family communication. The findings clearly indicate that differences between these two groups exist.

Not only do socio-oriented individuals watch more television, they employ the medium for a variety of social purposes not so used by their concept-oriented peers. Members of socio-oriented families agree that television is useful to them for interpersonal objectives which range from structuring their activities and talk patterns (the *environmental* and *regulative* functions) to uses of the medium for more complex relational purposes (*communication facilitation, affiliation/avoidance, social learning,* and *competence/ dominance*). Family members from concept-oriented homes, on the other hand, reported that, with few exceptions, television is not useful to them as a social resource.

In some cases, the social uses of television which were *not* reported as useful by socio-oriented audience members were the ones which were said to be used by family members who are concept oriented. For example, socio-oriented family members reported that they did not use television for the transmission of values, for regulating the experience of other family members via gatekeeping, or for exercising parental authority. These same social uses were among the few uses which correlated positively with concept orientation scores.

The most dramatic contrast between socio- and concept-oriented audience members was in their attitude toward television as a means for facilitating communication. Socio-oriented individuals agreed that all of the various strategies which comprise this component of the typology were useful to them. Concept-oriented family members were particularly strong in their personal rejection of these behaviors as a basis for family communication. The findings clearly demonstrate that family members from the two orientations disagree regarding the utility of television for providing an informational and emotional foundation from which to build satisfactory interpersonal communication at home.

The principal findings of this study are theoretically consistent with what is known about the two family communication orientations. The data provide additional empirical evidence which helps reveal the nature of contrasting media habits which occur where styles of interpersonal communication differ. Television is used by socio-oriented family members to help construct an actively interdependent communicative environment. Uses of television for various affiliative purposes, for example, were characteristic of socio-oriented individuals who have been shown to be agreeable and supportive in their interactions. Socio-oriented persons, who adopt each other's television habits (positive parental modeling for news and entertainment programs), were also found in the present study to model social behavior seen on television and to use television as a social learning device generally. The medium is also used by socio-oriented persons as a resource for conversational topics and for providing a desirable social activity – the viewing experience.

The socio-oriented family member apparently accepts television as an important part of the communication environment at home and uses the medium to further interpersonal goals. Although socio-oriented family members (especially parents) *submit* to television by watching it a lot and admit that it plays significant roles in their interpersonal behavior, they also claim to *use* it often and in various ways as a resource for constructing their desired social realities at home.

Despite previous research which indicated that socio-oriented families engage in parental control and punishment, the unwillingness of socio-oriented parents to regulate viewing or use television in order to exercise authority at home, however, indicates that the medium is not a tool used indiscriminately for all social purposes. The fact that socio-oriented fathers and mothers were shown to be heavy viewers of television may help explain their reluctance to use the medium in a restrictive way.

Concept-oriented family members claim more independence from the visual medium. Their high regard for individual expression, debate and discussion of ideas, and personal achievement may inhibit excessive amounts of television viewing. The rejection of nearly all the social uses of television by these family members seems to reflect extreme disregard for television as a significant contributor to family communication. The few uses of television which concept-oriented individuals say they employ conform to the findings of previous research. They utilize the medium in order to transmit family values, to regulate the children's experiences, and to facilitate arguments, actions which are concerned more with ideas than with social relationships.

Early research on the media habits of concept-oriented audience members demonstrated that they have a guarded attitude toward television. They exercise control over the medium, interpret programs, and watch more for information than for fantasy. They refrain from identifying with violent characters and draw a distinction between television characters and real-world persons. Not surprisingly, then, concept-oriented family members, for the most part, rejected the utility of television as a device for establishing, sustaining, or improving social relations at home. To participate significantly in social behavior where television plays a major role apparently would have been inconsistent with their overall attitude toward the medium.

Several of the social uses of television are not obvious behaviors and may never have been thought about or understood by the respondents. These subtle, unconscious influences have been termed media's 'latent functions' (Katz *et al.* 1974) and may only be uncovered and documented by ethnographic research. Further, some family members may not admit certain uses of television since manipulative intent on the part of the user could be inferred from several of the items. None the less, these survey data clearly indicate that audience members do recognize the utility of television as a social resource and that family communication patterns effectively predict differential use of the medium for a wide range of interpersonal objectives.

This chapter was originally published in *Communication Research*, 7, 3, 1980.

REFERENCES

Adoni, H. (1979) 'The functions of mass media in the political socialization of adolescents', *Communication Research* 6, 1: 84–106.

Blumler, J. G. (1979) 'The role of theory in uses and gratifications studies', *Communication Research* 6, 1: 9–36.

―――― and Katz, E. (1974) *The Uses of Mass Communications: Current Perspectives on Gratifications Research, Beverly Hills, CA: Sage.*

Chaffee, S. H., McLeod, J. M., and Atkin, C. K. (1971) 'Parental influences on adolescent media use', *American Behavioral Scientist* 14, 4: 323–40.

―――――, McLeod, J. M., and Wackman, D. B. (1966) 'Family communication and political socialization', paper presented to Association for Education in Journalism, Iowa City, Iowa.

―――――, McLeod, J. M., and Wackman, D. B. (1973) 'Family communication patterns and adolescent political participation', in J. Dennis (ed.) *Socialization to Politics*, New York: Wiley.

Katz, E., Blumler, J. G., and Gurevitch, M. (1974) 'Uses of mass communication by the individual', in W. P. Davison and F. T. C. Yu (eds) *Mass Communication Research*, New York: Praeger.

Lull, J. (1980) 'The social uses of television', *Human Communication Research* 6, 3: 197–209.

McLeod, J. M., Atkin, C. K., and Chaffee, S. H. (1972) 'Adolescents, parents and television use: self-report and other-report measures from the Wisconsin sample', in G. A. Comstock and E. A. Rubinstein (eds) *Television and Social Behavior*, Washington, D.C.: United States Government Printing Office.

―――――, Chaffee, S. H., and Wackman, D. B. (1967) 'Family communication: an updated report', paper presented to the Association for Education in Journalism, Boulder, Co.

McQuail, D., Blumler, J. G., and Brown, J. R. (1972) 'The television audience: a revised perspective', in D. McQuail (ed.) *Sociology of Mass Communication*, Harmondsworth, England: Penguin Books.

Nordenstreng, K. (1970) 'Comments on "gratification research" in broadcasting', *Public Opinion Quarterly* 34, 2: 130–2.

Swanson, D. L. (1979) 'Political communication research and the uses and gratifications model', *Communication Research* 6, 1: 37–53.

Ward, L. S. (1968) 'Some effects of the structure of relationships on interpersonal behavior in the dyad', doctoral dissertation, University of Wisconsin-Madison.

4 A rules approach to the study of television and society

Research on the structures and processes of mass communication – few sources and many receivers engaged in mediated, symbolic activity – began when most communication and sociological researchers were applying new quantitative methods impelled by probabilistic theoretical models in order to measure the 'variables' they believed were at work. The major themes of mass communication research emerged through the years from a positivist perspective that regards human communication as activity caused by fundamental laws of behavior. This epistemological framework has endured for several decades of mass communication research despite the inability of investigators in the field to produce empirical findings that achieve convincing evidence of *lawful* effects or human uses of the mass media.

Temporal differences, the influence of varying contexts, and the ability of human beings to phenomenologically invent transcendent courses of action are all factors that make communicative activity unique and difficult to measure or predict. None the less, probabilistic cause and effect theoretical models and their accompanying measurement procedures will surely remain useful as research tools for various important aspects of basic human activity, including quantifiable forms of audience behavior such as consumer habits or political activity measured in relation to media exposure. However, more complex features of audience behavior are less amenable to the methodological and analytical assumptions and procedures characteristic of most mass communication research. Mass media audiences create a wide variety of actions at micro- and macrosocial levels that cannot be easily categorized, aggregated, or condensed to meet the demands of parsimony and elegance typical of commonly used regression or path analytic predictive models.

In part because many communication scholars had been disappointed by the unsatisfactory explanatory power of traditional theories and methods, considerable interest was expressed when 'communication rules' – an alternative theoretical perspective on human communication – was introduced to the field in the 1970s (Cushman 1977; Cushman and Pearce 1977; Cushman and Whiting 1972; Pearce 1973). According to the rules conception, *human communication is made possible* by the normative interaction of individuals who *choose* particular verbal and nonverbal actions in order to forge meaning consensually and to negotiate simultaneously the procedures that can be employed in the use of symbols to construct social reality (Cushman and Whiting 1972). These central elements of communication – defining the content of interaction and developing procedures that can be used in order to negotiate meaning – are activities that interlocutors create and modify. They are not causally determined but are the *practical* outcomes of the interaction of specific communications objectives and contexts (Cushman 1977). Further, rules do not exist solely in face-to-face exchanges. Rules can also help explain the relationship between components of mediated symbolic communication systems.

The purpose of this writing is to provide a framework for the fruitful analysis of mass media audience behavior using a communication rules approach. This will be accomplished by first discussing the theoretical characteristics of the rules perspective and its relevance to the study of human interaction. Next, communication rules will be defined uniquely in a manner appropriate for conducting mass communication research at two levels of interaction – the family and the society. Finally, the potential contribution of the rules perspective for building mass communication theory will be discussed in a way that synthesizes empirical descriptions of audience activity with critical accounts of media's ideological roles.

THE RULES PERSPECTIVE IN COMMUNICATION

Each social actor comes to a communication experience equipped with a set of normative rules that constitute the individual's referential repertoire and his or her understanding of how meaning is derived through symbolic exchange. Observable patterns of rule use subsequently emerge during interaction and help create 'order and regularity in the communication process . . . by governing and guiding the communicative transaction' (Cushman and Whiting 1972: 228–9). Rules are varied and complex rather than unified (Toulmin 1974). Further, 'complex patterns of interpersonal communication require the concept of hierarchically ordered contracts, consisting of a few fundamental rules, several sets of rules governing interaction in specific situations, and switching cues used to move from one subset to another' (Pearce 1974: 160).

Communication rules are useful to social actors as practical inventions. The social actor chooses to engage in particular communications in order to accomplish certain goals. Interactants abide by a set of consensually understood rules in order to achieve those goals.

The rules perspective in communication does *not* require that researchers provide behavioral explanations based on temporal causality. Instead, examination of episodes in which rules are present allows the researcher to find 'general and specific patterns which provide the basis for a scientific explanation and prediction of human behavior, keeping in mind that the scientific explanations will appeal less to law-like regularities and more to rule-governed choices' (Cushman and Whiting 1972: 227). Still, one approach to discovering rules is to observe the 'regularity of their occurrence' in human interaction (Fisher 1978: 76).

A 'standardized usage' of rules takes place when participants in communication systems recognize, understand, and employ a common set of rules in order to interact normatively (Cappella 1972; Cushman and Pearce 1977). While some rules of interaction are socially and culturally understood and practiced by a wide range of users, other more intricate forms of rule-based interactions take place in dyads, families, and other social units that share unique methods of symbolic interaction. The diverse and idiosyncratic use of rules by social actors may inhibit external validation of any particular rule. None the less, classes or categories of rule-based behavior can be formed and may provide the basis for meaningful generalization.

Advocates of the rules perspective have clearly focused on the interactional nature of communication. The assumptions that underlie rules accommodate a realization by communication theorists that human interaction is a rich and complex symbol-exchanging activity characterized by phenomenological choice and contextual embeddedness. Communications' constitutive rules are further complicated by their developmental character (Ervin-Tripp 1973). Still rules are central to what social actors do when they communicate in all contexts and stages.

According to Cushman (1977), social groups must regulate consensus to co-ordinate human behavior. Rules *structure* human communication as interactants attempt to achieve this objective. The functioning and adaptive human use of rules is the *process* of communication (Cushman 1977). Although interactants may not desire to understand or be understood at all times (Pearce 1973), various parties to a communication event must at least co-ordinate their utterances in order to create or sustain meaning (accurate or not) and achieve a procedure for doing so. The communication researcher must then 'explicate the powerful mechanisms which give rise to rule behaviors and determine the logical and empirical conditions under which each type of rule regularity might be expected' (Cushman 1977: 39).

The assumptions that are said to underlie any particular rules approach, however, are contestable. For instance, a major theoretical issue that faces rules researchers is the degree to which communication rules and the very social structures they help create should be considered homogeneous or heterogeneous. The conception of rules as operative within a homogeneous social order presumes that individual actors already share common understandings (rules) of communications. The researcher must then 'produce microscopic descriptions of the rules actors use . . . within an assumed homogeneous social order' (Donohue, Cushman, and Nofsinger 1980: 6). Pike referred to this approach as an 'emic' descriptive process whereby the researcher examines the 'particular function of . . . particular events in (a) particular culture as it and it alone is structured' (Pike 1966: 157).

Heterogeneous rule systems, on the other hand, presume that 'people communicate to resolve *differing* conceptions of their mutual problems' (Donohue *et al.* 1980: 6, italics added). The researcher analyzes how human communication is used as a resource for behavioral co-ordination and problem-solving. This perspective coincides with Pike's 'etic' form of description whereby human action is cross-culturally observed and compared from outside any particular communication system. Sigman (1980) has discussed the homogeneity/heterogeneity issue in ethnographic rules research in terms of the 'isomorphy' of rule structure that obtains in varying social contexts.

Although great interest in communication rules has been expressed lately, rules certainly have not been defined or applied in any standardized way in social research. Toulmin (1974) developed a fundamental seven-component taxonomy. Cushman (1977) modified and elaborated Toulmin's list for purposes of conducting interpersonal communication research. Shimanoff (1980) reviewed numerous rules typologies within a variety of academic disciplines and attempted to explain subtle differences in the multitude of rule types that have been identified. She then proposed a rules taxonomy that she said combines the strengths of previous work. The rules framework that she presented demonstrates that rules exist at various levels of conscious awareness; that they may be primarily explicit or implicit; that they may be complied with or violated; and that social actors can reflect evaluatively upon the rule systems in which they are enmeshed (Shimanoff 1980: 125). Pearce (1980) reviewed what he considers to be the most productive communication rule types but concluded that no single approach is particularly compelling.

It may be impossible to explain parsimoniously the range of irregular events that constitute the whole of human communication by reference to any specific set of rules. None the less, there are three essential heuristic themes that emerge from each typology or review of communication rules. These rule types will be introduced briefly now and refined in later sections of this chapter.

First, some rules of human interaction occur in a seemingly automatic, regularly repeated manner with no evidence of social arbitration. They are *habits* that are often instituted by authority. These fundamental rules reveal status-related interpersonal behavior, sometimes exist as obligatory actions, and may carry negative sanctions when violated. Second, other rules involve human interaction that varies contextually within consensually understood boundaries or *parameters*. These rules are sometimes, but not always, consciously recognized and articulated. They govern social intercourse by defining what actions are appropriate within the latitudes of acceptable behavior. Third, a more complicated communication rules type incorporates a strategic dimension. In this case, social actors co-ordinate their symbolic exchanges according to informally understood rules that are exercised pragmatically in order to achieve some personal or interpersonal objective. These *tactical* rules are created by individuals, dyads, groups, and cultures in order to solve problems or realize goals.

The rules types that will frame the following discussion, therefore, are habitual, parametric, and tactical. These communication rules inhabit the interpersonal exchanges of families as they experience the mass media and the parasociocultural interactions that connect individual audience members to the institutional values and suggested behaviors routinely symbolized in media content. A major objective of this paper is to demonstrate the face validity, explanatory potential, and practicality of habitual, parametric, and tactical communication rules for the analysis of media audience activity in its micro- and macrointeractional contexts.

THE RULES PERSPECTIVE IN MASS COMMUNICATION

Rules of mass communication occupy two fundamental domains with respect to audience activity. While the kinds of rules that function in these differing spheres may be similar, their actual manifestations and the consequences they suggest are quite different. First, natural microinteractional media audiences, particularly *families*, can be analyzed as rule-oriented social units that consume media content. A researcher examines the empirical operations of family life in order to describe and explain what activities characterize audience members' relationships with one another as they experience television or any mass medium. Second, the *society* can be examined as a macrointeractional unit of analysis in mass communication. Cushman (1977) has recognized the possibility of such an application of communication rules. He points out that 'mass communication serves to coordinate human activity in regard to social and cultural institutions. . . . The content and procedural rules provide information about social institutions and prescribe the communication patterns for social roles' (Cushman 1977: 39). A researcher may employ a case-study approach to examine message-creation processes or content analysis to discover dominant themes of the culture and economy that reside in mass symbol systems.

The theoretical framework that will be developed below considers the unique contributions that television makes to audience members' construction of social reality at both levels. This will be accomplished by describing rule-patterned behaviors that help explain how television influences interpersonal communication and, in the larger sense, how the medium influences broad patterns of social and cultural activities. The communication rules conception, therefore, will be shown to apply to interpersonal communication where the focus is television and to audience members' collective interaction with television. Empirical data-gathering techniques are the chief methodological tools that can be employed to describe the former; critical methodologies as well as empirical approaches can be used to assess the latter.

VIEWING RULES IN THE FAMILY

Rules that families employ to regulate their experiences with television extend over a range of daily activities. These rules are sometimes codified; other times they are unstructured or unarticulated. They can be formal or informal and can be applied directly or indirectly. Rules for viewing may involve at least the amount of television viewed at home, the time when television is viewed, program content, the program selection process, activity which accompanies viewing, reward or punishment (social control rules), or media-related interpersonal strategies undertaken by family members.

Habitual rules

Behaviors that comprise this rule type are firmly established and regularly repeated classes of human activity. Habitual actions are distinguished from other rule types by the fact that they are not negotiated or modified interactively. Many habitual rules involve young children since they are frequent television viewers and some of their parents desire to control their behavior at least some of the time. Habitual rules are represented in patterns of routine human interaction, the bases of which are not likely to be questioned.

As young children grow to become active members of their home environments, they quickly learn the habitual rules of accepted behavior at home. These rules have been created by their parents and older siblings and constitute a normative environment that initially exists outside the young child's influence. All humans first occupy social environments where rules that confer meaning and style are already established. Indeed, some of the most painful emotional experiences in childhood occur when children learn that their first interpretations of reality or claims for desired styles of interaction are not shared by the older, more powerful members of the family.

Empirical researchers have produced conflicting findings about the extent to which parents impose nonnegotiable viewing rules of various types on their children. Lyle and Hoffman (1972) found that attempts to control viewing of tenth-grade children existed in less than 10 percent of their survey sample. Canavan (1974) reported that Australian parents 'exert little influence over their children's viewing' (p. 14). But Steiner (1963) and Bower (1973) found that about 40 percent of the American families they surveyed have 'definite' rules about the amount, time, or content of television viewing that is allowed. Bower also reported that about two-thirds of all families impose 'some control' over the viewing of their children who range in age from 4 to 12 years. Barcus (1969) also found that parents exercise significant control over viewing and that their styles for doing so were richly varied. The abundance of evidence suggests that the imposition of viewing rules is not uncommon and that these rules are not limited only to younger children. Habitual viewing rules regarding the timing and content of viewing may apply even more often to children who are nearly teenagers (Bower 1973). Bower explained this finding partly by suggesting that parents may use television as a babysitter for very young children and may actually be more restrictive of older children who do not have to be preoccupied with the medium.

Even after they develop distinct preferences for particular shows and genres of programs (Lyle and Hoffman 1972; Wartella 1979), gaining regular access to television is often problematic for children of various ages. Very young children may face a variety of obstacles in order to watch prime-time television if their parents habitually disallow night-time television viewing for them. Similarly, parents may habitually prevent viewing at certain times for older children since television may be thought to interfere with homework or other household responsibilities. Certain program themes also may be considered by parents to be irrevocably off-limits for preteenagers or teenagers.

Habitual rules do not always take the form of restrictions or guidelines imposed by authority figures on less powerful family members. For instance, some working parents assert jurisdictional rights to select television programs at night because it is their only opportunity for viewing during the week and becomes a nonnegotiable reward for employment (Lull 1976). Other habits may simply involve the repeated viewing of programs preferred by parents or older siblings. Under these circumstances, habitual rules come to be understood through the structured viewing experience (Barcus 1969). Parents' media habits may then become direct influences on children's media habits (Chaffee and Tims 1976), although empirical support for a modeling hypothesis from parent to child is not conclusive (Chaffee, McLeod, and Atkin 1971).

70   *Inside Family Viewing*

Parametric rules

Some human action unfolds under rule-governed conditions whereby only certain behavior is permitted within negotiable boundaries.
Like habits, an authority typically influences these actions. However, parametric rules differ from habitual rules in that interactants
have opportunities to choose alternative courses of behavior within
a range of permitted activities. The parameters refer to the limits
that are placed on the action. Parametric rules frame the interactive,
choice-making behaviors that are conducted by social actors in order
to accomplish immediate tasks. They serve no apparent purposes
that exceed the immediate communication context.

There are many television-related family interactions that fall into
this category. Perhaps the most common and clear example is the
negotiation of television program preferences or times for viewing.
Parameters can refer to choices that are allowed (times for viewing,
types of programs, particular programs) or to the kinds of contributions that can be made in the program-selection task since families construct a variety of rule-based methods for interactively choosing shows (Bower 1973; Lull 1978; Niven 1960; Wand 1968).

Some parametric program-selection rules favor the interests of
children. Because young children are often unable to compete verbally with older family members in discussions about television
viewing (Lull 1978), these family decisions, known as 'special rules',
bestow unique status on young children (Streicher and Bonney
1974). Another parametric approach is 'first-served' or 'calling' favorite shows (naming them early in the day as candidates for later
viewing). These procedures also sometimes work to the advantage
of younger viewers since they often are more preoccupied with
television viewing than other family members and are more likely
to activate the set or verbally claim their favorites before other
potential viewers do so (Streicher and Bonney 1974).

Parametric rules that influence the television viewing experience
are not limited to the program-selection process. Another set of
rule-governed activities constitute the 'rhythm of viewing', a concept
not unlike rhythms of dialogue – the nature of conversational flow
based on its normative character (Cappella 1979, 1980; Jaffee and
Feldstein 1970). For instance, television's regular commercial breaks
help establish routinized patterns of talk in front of the set. These
patterns may vary during different breaks but there is a general
understanding in many families that conversation during program
segments should not exceed unspecified limits in length (Lull 1976).

Another recent observational study found that children's responses to television advertising are parametrically rule-governed (Reid 1979). Parents in many homes controlled the range of children's behavioral expectations while viewing television commercials; the types and degree of parent–child conflict that can be stimulated by commercials; and the nature and length of interruptive activities that accompany viewing, particularly conversation and play.

Parametric rules pertain to many of the same areas of family television consumption as do habitual rules. Each rule type can be applied to the amount and time of viewing that is done by an individual or the group; to censorship of program content through selectivity or expurgation; to the program-selection process itself; and to the nature of the viewing experience. The crucial distinction between the rule types rests in the degree of authoritarian control that obtains. In habitual rules, authority figures (parents, siblings) impose nonnegotiable behavioral codes. Parametric rules, on the other hand, permit variation in human activity resulting from nego- tiation, but again the range of allowable behavioral alternatives is authoritatively prescribed.

Tactical rules

These rules appear in human interaction as attempts to achieve some personal or interpersonal objective that exists beyond the immediate context of media consumption. They are pragmatic means-to-end strategies devised by individuals, dyads, or groups in order to gain some objective that is typically more important and abstract than are the conditions and rewards of the situation at hand. They are frequently complex inventions and may not always be recognized or articulated by the interactants who are involved.

For instance, a man and woman may use television viewing as a pragmatic method for maintaining a satisfying relationship (Lull 1980a). To demonstrate this, a rules-based practical syllogism can be used to illustrate choice-making activity that immediately involves television, but ultimately involves the cultivation of interpersonal harmony. The tactic takes this general form: Person *A* desires to achieve *C*; in order for *A* to achieve *C*, s/he must do *B*; *A* sets herself/himself to do *B* (Cushman and Pearce 1977; von Wright 1962). Some idea of the specific goal of communication is needed in order to give meaning to a communication rules interpretation. The syllogism can be modeled with this simple example: A husband (*A*) desires to maintain marital harmony (*C*) with his wife; in order to do so, he determines that 'giving in' on certain television viewing (*B*) is a means to accomplish his goal. He (*A*) changes the channel to her favorite show (*B*). The fundamental criteria of the practical syllogism have been met and the result is deduced. In cases like this, television is used strategically by social actors as a resource for the accomplishment of particular interpersonal objectives. The activity is rule-based since the behavior is patterned and can be deduced from the pragmatic interaction of the television-viewing experience and the relational needs of the viewers.

Relationship maintenance is but one example of how rule-based, television-related communication can be used socially. Lull (1980a) has demonstrated that families use television for a wide range of social purposes in the general areas of communication facilitation, achieving the desired degree of interpersonal affiliation or avoidance, social learning, and demonstration of interpersonal competence or dominance. Further, television is used as a social resource differentially by families in ways consistent with their overall styles of family communication (Lull 1980b). 'Concept-oriented' parents, for instance, are more likely than 'socio-oriented' parents to use television in order to exercise authority over their children or to transmit values to them. These rule-governed social uses of television are uniquely tactical. One purpose for parental regulation of television viewing under these circumstances is to achieve some interpersonal objective (demonstration of competence; inculcation of desired values) that is removed from the exigencies of the immediate viewing experience.

Tactical rule use also appears in the form of 'social-control rules' whereby television viewing is given as a reward or punishment (Fry and McCain 1980). These television rules were found to be related to other activities and regulations in the home and were also influenced by patterns of family communication. Protective families (socio orientation) were more concerned than concept families with social control rules. Also, parents with high concept orientations had more 'content discussion' rules than did parents with low concept orientations. Blood (1961) also made empirical connections between parental control of television viewing and other aspects of family life, finding that tactical rules that involve television differ by social class. Upper-class families controlled television more than did lower-class families and used reasoning as a method for doing so. Lower-class families relied more upon direct methods of intervention.

Rules enter family interaction in ways that define the activity as communication. Habitual, parametric, and tactical activities carry with them implications that surpass the choosing and watching of television shows. Through television-related interaction, family members also learn relational realities – meaning that takes form in the interpersonal uses and consequences of communication rules. Features of interaction such as interpersonal power may emerge during rule-based exchanges that perhaps even influence interlocuters' self-concepts (Cushman 1977).

VIEWING RULES IN SOCIETY

A rules analysis of society suggests that human action regarding social and cultural institutions is co-ordinated through mass communication. In order to demonstrate how this works, the rules framework constructed here will consider (1) the nature of sociocultural consensus sought by media sources, (2) who the advocates of consensus are and what their methods are, and (3) the societal implications of massive symbolic communication.

The concept of social consensus presupposes that some systematic form of interaction takes place between television's human senders and receivers and that audience members' collective responses to media are patterned. Various strains of mass communication research have indicated that audience members, even those who live alone, develop a 'relationship' with television. Years ago, Horton and Wohl (1956) observed that audience members interact 'parasocially' with television characters and seemingly become acquainted, in their own minds, with the medium's stars. Noble (1975) has shown that television viewers often 'identify' with actors and actresses on the screen, or 'recognize' them and carry on a kind of mental interchange during viewing. Television soap operas are particularly likely to cause their audiences to become 'involved' (Compesi 1980). The media 'uses and gratifications' literature reviewed by Katz *et al.* (1974) is replete with ways that audience members use the medium for fantasy escape and for identifying with selected heroes and heroines. The interaction that occurs is primarily an investment of interest or emotion by the audience member into the lives and situations that are portrayed on the screen. A small number of viewers formalize their responses to television shows by sending fan mail or complaints to the actors, production companies, television stations, networks, or regulatory agencies.

Less directly, but more powerfully, audience members also

respond to television in the aggregate by their consumer purchases, political activities, expectations regarding the sociocultural environment, and imitative performance of social roles learned from program content. These processes are formed and reinforced, in part, by repeated exposure to the dominant ideological themes that appear on television.

By examining the content of television and the human activity that surrounds use of the medium, a mass communication researcher can analyze broad themes of social behavior that reflect conformity to rule-governed choices as well as pragmatic strategies of consumption and social action. Societal level rules, therefore, are more parametric and tactical than they are habitual. It is difficult to conceptualize a nonnegotiable, habitual relationship between a media source and viewer since no *direct* controls over the viewing experience can be imposed by authorities external to the viewing location.

Parametric rules

Institutions that stand to profit by the widespread distribution of information via television construct and maintain message systems that ultimately cultivate enormous audiences, supplying them with a narrow and predictable range of behavioral predispositions (Gerbner 1973). Consequently, the rule-based choices that viewers exercise are limited (in terms of the television-viewer relationship) to the alternatives permitted by authority – corporate interests that directly control the content of advertising messages and indirectly manage the content of entertainment programs, newscasts, and public affairs shows. The messages that are offered to audience members are value-laden in their surface persuasive content and in the more subtle ideas they transmit through subtextual cues and the technical structuring of imagery (Fiske and Hartley 1978; Hall 1975).

True to the rules conception, television viewers choose to watch varying program content. However, only a tightly controlled range of program elements, each of which teaches the language of the socioeconomic system and its corresponding cultural assumptions, is available for viewing. The actual choosing of program materials, willingness to accept or reject the premises explicitly or implicitly stated in program content, and varying behavioral responses to these notions following viewing constitute at least the appearance of negotiation, a fundamental criterion for rule-bound activity to be regarded as parametric.

There is considerable empirical evidence to firmly indicate that the audience collectively responds to television in ways the controlling interests desire. It is true that audience members have the option to turn off the television set; to disregard or refute the content of themes repeatedly portrayed on television; to escape the influence of national advertising through alternative consumer activity; and to elect political candidates who have not appeared regularly on the visual medium. Every television set has an off switch; every audience member has potential access to streams of information that conflict with television's messages; most stores carry products that are not advertised on television; and electoral ballots bear the names and party affiliations of candidates who do not receive much attention from the media. Still, Americans watch television now more than ever before; the medium effectively sets the agenda for a great deal of conversation and behavior that takes place during viewing and following exposure; national advertising campaigns frequently achieve enormous financial success in direct relation to sponsored imagery; and mainstream political parties and their candidates continue to dominate the American political system (Comstock *et al.* 1978).

These facts support the fundamental critique that powerful ideological consortia exercise significant control over the activities of national audiences by exploiting an apparent human attraction to light, nonpolitical entertainment (lowest common denominator programming); by selecting and excluding topics for interpretive treatment in entertainment programming and in news content (censorship); by advertising brand names and product groups that perpetuate the economic viability of entrenched industry even in the face of resistance (e.g. the automobile industry v. potential popular support for efficient mass transit systems); by legitimizing cultural values and lifestyles supportive of corporate economic imperatives by means of stereotyping; and by actively lobbying against attempts by splinter political parties and candidates to gain access to television via spot messages, public affairs shows, equal treatment in national news, and opportunities for the presentation of minority views on televised debates.

Opportunities for qualitative feedback from individual audience members to sources of programming are vague and indirect. The negotiation of parametric rule-based activity involving the principle interactants – sources of television programming and audience members – is similarly indirect. The individual audience member cannot alter the rules of mediated interaction but can only choose to accept or reject the messages as they exist. The proven tendency is for most audience members to stay within the prescribed parameters and exercise choices from the range of allowable alternatives. There have been isolated instances of collective negative feedback from audiences to centralized programming sources (other than the ratings) in the form of program or product boycotts. However, these actions typically have been short-lived and directed toward specific programs, products, or brand names rather than toward essential problems in the economic system itself.

Tactical rules

These strategic communicative activities were shown to play an important role in family communication. The importance should again be emphasized at the societal level, where audience members undertake culturally patterned strategic transactions with sources of media programming. It will be recalled from the previous discussion that these rule-based practical inventions are created in order to achieve an abstract purpose that is removed from the immediate viewing context. At the societal level, tactical rules of communication are employed in order to reward media sources with profits, and viewers with personal or social accomplishments or promises of such.

The practical relationship that exists between the advertiser and the viewer-consumer may most clearly illuminate the point. Through advertising, television incessantly suggests 'solutions' to human 'problems' in the form of strategies for social action. A fundamental purpose of advertising, of course, is to publicize the availability and desirability of products (solutions) that individuals believe they need (personal transportation, beauty aids, financial 'services', etc.). By selecting one brand of cosmetics over another in order to achieve the desired physical appearance (a suggested corporate solution for the 'need' to be attractive), for instance, the viewer-consumer perpetuates the product group represented in the purchase through tactical rule-based behavior – responding to a social strategy suggested through advertising. Television may also create 'false needs', then suggest methods by which they can be satisfied (Marcuse 1964).

Television viewers may be convinced to purchase advertised products in order to acquire some degree of personal security that greatly exceeds the objective capabilities of the product. A recent national television commercial campaign, for instance, showed a young man standing next to his new Toyota automobile while several attractive young women walked past him adoringly. Noticing the female attention, the man asks rhetorically: 'Is it me or my Toyota?' At the conclusion of the commercial one of the admirers answers: 'It's your Toyota, silly.' Clearly, the advertisement was designed to sell much more than personal transportation. The viewer who is influenced by this message may regard the purchase of the new car as a strategy that can facilitate personal or interpersonal objectives. If this behavior is patterned across the culture, advertising sources and viewer-consumers successfully engage in large-scale, mediated, tactical interaction that may also help promote consumption-dependent values in everyday, unmediated social interaction.

Children are special targets for suggested tactical social action that involves media solutions (e.g. peer acceptance). During the first few years of their experiences with television, children are unable to identify the motives of television advertisers (Ward and Wackman 1973; Wartella 1979). In later stages of development they begin to recognize advertisers' intentions; however, recognition does not imply rejection of them. While some children may express knowledge of advertisers' motives to researchers, or to each other in their conversations, they are constantly exposed to hundreds of thousands of messages that encourage strategic patterns of consumption and social action supportive of the objectives of the few corporations that are able to purchase network advertising. The long-term success of several advertised products directed toward children attests to the ability of these culture producers effectively to persuade the youth market (Melody 1973).

The advertising examples are only the most obvious representatives of tactical rules at the societal level that involve television content. Practical methods suggested by television for personal or social success are also evident directly in the story lines of dramatic programs; in occurrences that are selected for treatment in news programming; and in the subtle, subtextual lessons of television programming generally. The visual medium's symbolic content is one version of the normative constitution of culture – its rules – that is transmitted to a larger audience than is regularly exposed to any other centralized message source. Elements of the reality portrayed on television subsequently become resources for determining the boundaries within which the society should proceed; for choosing popular courses of social action; and for calculating specific means-to-ends strategies such as the rule-based problem-solving activities discussed above. Large-scale social consensus is achieved in the process, and the result, in the traditional sociological sense, is mass communication.

RULES IN MASS COMMUNICATION THEORY

Communication rules is a theoretical perspective that directs researchers' attention to patterns of human activity resulting from choices made by social actors as they define their realities and construct methods of interaction. Choices are made in response to the practical exigencies of particular micro- or macrointeractional contexts and are strongly influenced by normative expectations. Communication rules are the stabilizing agents of social intercourse which, cumulatively, become the forceful, consensually shared linkages of a normative society. The patterned breaking of communication rules leads to the gradual restructuring of sociocultural norms.

Rules exist in a variety of forms at the family and societal levels of human interaction. When analyzed from the rules perspective, mass communication is fundamentally defined as interactional, consensus-seeking, choice-making activity undertaken within specifiable boundaries and with particular tasks in mind by small groups and by society. Rule construction and use are wholly practical activities. They do not function in the probabilistic, cause-and-effect manner envisioned by the proponents of scientific laws explanations of human behavior.

The major themes of television research, including the medium's effects on children, media gratifications, agenda-setting, and the construction of leisure-time activities, can all be addressed from the rules perspective. In this paper, communication rules were shown to inhabit many specific aspects of the human experience with television, including (1) the choosing of programs, (2) activities that accompany viewing, (3) defining interpersonal relationships in the home, (4) socialization to values prescribed by the medium's controlling economic interests, and (5) consumer and political behavior.

In the family, the researcher can locate patterns of rule-based, media-related activity by noting the origins, clustering of definitional characteristics, and frequency of occurrence of repeated, pertinent actions. Habitual rules can often be distinguished from parametric rules by observing and/or inquiring about the degree of negotiation that inheres in media-related behavior. It must be kept in mind, however, that some habitual rules are implicit human activities that have simply derived phenomenologically from the circumstances of previous viewing experiences. Tactical rules can be observed and analyzed in terms of the pragmatic objectives they serve and the results they attain. These often complex rules are found in extended interpersonal networks where television, or any mass medium, plays a role.

Communication rules can be used not only as a framework to help explain audience behavior in terms of the routines and pragmatics of family communication, but also in terms of viewers' collective, mediated interactions involving contact with themes supportive of the dominant economy. Communication rules, therefore, make a necessary connection between the concerns of empirical mass communication researchers who examine media's roles in human interaction and critical researchers who focus their analyses on media content and its relation to domestic and international economic theory and history (Ewen 1976; Gitlin 1979, 1980; Hall 1979; Kellner 1979; Murdock and Golding 1979; Sallach 1974; Schiller 1973, 1976). The rules perspective provides a theoretical link between human behavior that occurs in natural social contexts and the impact of the ideological motifs that television viewers receive from institutional sources of information about the existence, priorities, values, and relationships implicit in the economic and cultural order (Gerbner 1973). An important potential contribution of communication rules as a theoretical approach to the study of audience behavior, therefore, is that it weaves together issues of media criticism with empirical accounts of the relationship between audience members and sources of television programming. Empirical and critical approaches can be regarded within the rules framework as complementary rather than competitive evidentiary paths for theory development.

Importantly, the rules perspective promotes analysis of audience members as active agents in the creation of reality. The seeming contradiction in the mass communication literature between 'direct effects' and 'uses and gratifications' research is approached productively from the rules perspective. The conceptualization of the audience member as an active agent in communication (Katz *et al.* 1974) is firmly rooted in many of the features of the rules perspective, including choice-making, negotiation, transcendence, and strategy construction. Within the rules formulation the individual is not considered to be simply a respondent to interpersonal or mediated messages, but instead as an inspired, functioning person who acts willingly and with intelligence upon the manifest symbolic environment.

None the less, these actions are undertaken by audience members within familial and cultural surroundings where suggested courses of action are repeatedly advocated by power figures who occupy the locations. While broad patterns of human behavior are influenced by the parameters or tactics suggested by authority, individuals can none the less choose to ignore, alter, or disobey communication rules (Shimanoff 1980). These functions of evaluation, modification, and transcendence are unique to rules *vis-à-vis* scientific laws and seem well suited for development of a communication theory that takes into account the natural variability and dynamism of human action. Since the rules perspective combines interpersonal relations and ideological processes in a single analytic framework, theory can be developed at both levels that considers the audience member as a choice-maker who is not irreversibly trapped within communicational and cultural boundaries but is repeatedly advised to stay within them. The rules perspective permits meaningful analysis of phenomena in a manner that obviates conflict in what is perhaps the major, on-going theoretical issue that faces mass communication researchers: the direction of influence (persuasive 'effect' v. personal/interpersonal 'uses'). The audience member can simultaneously use and experience the effects of mass media.

Mass communication is a unique form of human interaction that has understandably suffered from lack of a parsimonious, organizing theoretical principle. Since the interpersonal activities that surround television viewing appear on the surface to differ greatly from audience members' personal connections with mediated symbol systems and their referents, it is hardly surprising that no single theory of mass communication has evolved. This paper has attempted to demonstrate that phenomena inherent in micro- and macrolevels of television-related activity have important similarities and can be commonly addressed as communication rules. Analyses of mass communication processes framed from the rules perspective should emphasize description and explanation of human television-related activity since the complexity of many of the events under study and the persistent human tendency to modify and alter even routine communication make valid prediction unlikely. The findings of previous empirical research in mass communication amply demonstrate this limitation.

Research methods appropriate for rule-based mass communication theory building are not limited to any one type. Descriptive empirical techniques such as survey research can be used to document family interactions and patterns of consumer and political behavior. In order to locate or verify the rules of human communication, however, the social researcher may want to study instances of natural interaction at first hand. The value of naturalistic, observational audience research has been recognized and discussed by scholars who represent a wide range of theoretical and methodological interests. Shimanoff (1980) has recommended naturalistic observation in order to increase generalizability of rule use and to identify 'tacit rules'. Katz, the renowned empiricist, has suggested a case-study approach to the investigation of audience behavior by entering the 'natural habitat of the viewer' (Katz 1977: 61). Critical theorist Gitlin has argued for the 'ethnography of audiences' (Gitlin 1979: 253). Blumer has urged researchers to study media audiences at home to learn how people symbolically interact with each other and with the media in order to 'forge definitions inside their experience' (Blumer 1969: 191). Historical and content analytic techniques have been productively applied to the ideological issues.

Although this discussion has emphasized the rule-based activities of audience members, there are rules for writers of television programs too. In a book about television industry, Brown (1971) referred to the 'rules' for writing a successful program. Rules for writers are not formulated as a result of direct contact with receivers of the messages. Instead, they derive from interpretations of audience ratings made by officials at the television networks (Cantor 1980). Network officials censor on-going programs when the rules are broken and prevent the airing of new shows that fail to adhere to the norm. Other rules govern the symbolic exchange between the various interpersonal components in the production of television programs. These rules direct action in locations where writers collectively compose their stories; on studio floors where shows are produced; in meeting places where representatives from production houses and the networks negotiate contracts; in decision-making meetings within the networks; and in the interaction that takes place between the networks and their affiliates. Each of these rule-oriented environments helps form the symbolic link between sources of television programming and their viewers.

Rules research in mass communication can examine media sources and audiences as heterogeneous entities engaged in mediated interaction. For instance, Shimanoff (1980) has recommended that mass media researchers examine the conversational

82 *Inside Family Viewing*

rules that appear in television program scripts in relation to the rules
of naturalistic conversation in order to compare writers' assumptions
about social interaction with what actually happens. In general,
implications of communication rules for media production, regulation, and evaluation may have theoretical merit that is as important as the audience studies that have been discussed in this writing.

Interpersonal and parasociocultural activities that involve television can all be scrutinized within the general conception of communication rules and, specifically, within the analytic framework
that has been advanced in this paper. These operations can be
further related to the theoretical interests held by researchers who
study mass communication from cognitive, social, cultural, or critical perspectives. For purposes of producing research of enduring
value to scholars of mass communication, the rules perspective may
prove to be at least as useful as scientific laws or the purely interpretive approaches.

This chapter was originally published in *Human Communication
Research*, 9, 1, 1982.

REFERENCES

Barcus, F. E. (1969) 'Parental influence on children's television viewing',
    Television Quarterly 8, 1: 63–73.
Blood, R. O. (1961) 'Social class and family control of television viewing',
    Merrill-Palmer Quarterly of Behavior and Development 7, 4: 205–22.
Blumer, H. (1969) *Symbolic Interactionism*, Englewood Cliffs, NJ:
    Prentice-Hall.
Bower, R. T. (1973) *Television and the Public*, New York: Holt, Rinehart
    & Winston.
Brown, L. (1971) *Television: The Business Behind the Box*, New York:
    Harcourt Brace Jovanovich.
Canavan, K. (1974) 'Children's television viewing habits and parental
    control', *Education News* 14, 1: 12–19.
Cantor, M. (1980) *Prime-time Television: Content and Control*, Beverly
    Hills, CA: Sage Publications.
Cappella, J. N. (1972) 'The functional prerequisites of intentional
    communication systems', *Philosophy and Rhetoric* 5, 4: 231–74.
_____ (1979) 'Talk-silence sequences in informal conversations I', *Human
    Communication Research* 6, 1: 3–17.
_____ (1980) 'Talk-silence sequences in informal conversations II',
    Human Communication Research 7, 2: 130–45.
Chaffee, S. H., McLeod, J. M., and Atkin, C. K. (1971) 'Parental
    influences on adolescent media use', *American Behavioral Scientist*
    14, 2: 149–72.

_____ and Tims, A. (1976) 'Interpersonal factors in adolescent television use', *Journal of Social Issues* 2, 2: 98–115.

Compesi, R. (1980) 'Gratifications of daytime TV serial viewers', *Journalism Quarterly* 57, 2: 155–8.

Comstock, G. A., Chaffee, S. H., Katzman, N., McCombs, M., and Roberts, D. (1978) *Television and Human Behavior*, New York: Columbia University Press.

Cushman, D. (1977) 'The rules perspective as a theoretical basis for the study of human communication', *Communication Quarterly* 25, 1: 30–45.

_____ and Whiting, G. (1972) 'An approach to communication theory: Toward consensus on rules', *Journal of Communication* 22, 3: 217–38.

_____ and Pearce, W. B. (1977) 'Generality and necessity in three types of communication theory', *Human Communication Research* 3, 4: 344–53.

Donohue, W. A., Cushman, D. P., and Nofsinger, R. E. (1980) 'Creating and confronting social order: a comparison of rules perspectives', *Western Journal of Speech Communication* 44, 1: 5–19.

Ervin-Tripp, S. (1973) *Language Acquisition and Communicative Choice*, Stanford, CA: Stanford University Press.

Ewen, S. (1976) *Captains of Consciousness*, New York: McGraw-Hill.

Fisher, A. (1978) *Perspectives on Human Communication*, New York: Macmillan.

Fiske, J. and Hartley, J. (1978) *Reading Television*, London: Methuen.

Fry, D. L. and McCain, T. A. (1980) 'Controlling children's television viewing: predictors of family television rules and their relationship to family communication patterns', paper presented to Association for Education in Journalism, Boston.

Gerbner, G. (1973) 'Cultural indicators: the third voice', in G. Gerbner, L. Gross, and W. Melody (eds) *Communications Technology and Social Policy: Understanding the Cultural Revolution*, New York: Wiley.

Gitlin, T. (1979) 'Prime-time ideology: the hegemonic process in television entertainment', *Social Problems* 26, 4: 251–66.

_____ (1980) *The Whole World Is Watching: Mass Media and the Making and Unmaking of the New Left*, Berkeley, CA: University of California Press.

Hall, S. (1975) 'The structured communication of events', in *Getting the Message Across*, Paris: UNESCO.

_____ (1979) 'Culture, the media, and the "ideological effect" ', in J. Curran, M. Gurevitch, and J. Woollacott (eds) *Mass Communication and Society*, Beverly Hills, CA: Sage Publications.

Horton, D. and Wohl, R. R. (1956) 'Mass communication and para-social interaction', *Psychiatry* 19, 4: 215–29.

Jaffe, J. and Feldstein, S. (1970) *Rhythms of Dialogue*, New York: Academic Press.

Katz, E. (1977) *Social Research on Broadcasting*, London: British Broadcasting Corporation.

_____ Blumler, J. G., and Gurevitch, M. (1974) 'Uses of mass communication by the individual', in W. P. Davison and F. T. C. Yu (eds)ˊ *Mass Communication Research*, New York: Praeger.

Kellner, D. (1979) 'TV, ideology, and emancipatory popular culture', *Socialist Review* 9, 1: 13–53.

Lull, J. (1976) 'Mass media and family communication: an ethnography of audience behavior', doctoral dissertation, University of Wisconsin-Madison.

_____ (1978) 'Choosing television programs by family vote', *Communication Quarterly* 26, 1: 53–7.

_____ (1980a) 'The social uses of television', *Human Communication Research*, 6, 3: 197–209.

_____ (1980b) 'Family communication patterns and the social uses of television', *Communication Research* 7, 3: 319–34.

Lyle, J. and Hoffman, H. R. (1972) 'Children's use of television and other media', in E. A. Rubinstein, G. A. Comstock, and J. P. Murray (eds) *Television and Social Behavior, 4: Television in Day-to-Day Life*, Washington, DC: United States Government Printing Office.

Marcuse, H. (1964) *One-Dimensional Man*, Boston: Beacon Press.

Melody, W. (1973) *Children's Television*, New Haven, CT: Yale University Press.

Murdock, G. and Golding, P. (1979) 'Capitalism, communication, and class relations', in J. Curran, M. Gurevitch, and J. Woollacott (eds) *Mass Communication and Society*, Beverly Hills, CA: Sage Publications.

Niven, H. (1960) 'Who in the family selects the TV program?', *Journalism Quarterly* 37, 2: 110–11.

Noble, G. (1975) *Children in Front of the Small Screen*, London: Constable.

Pearce, W. B. (1974) 'Consensual rules in interpersonal communication: a reply to Cushman and Whiting', *Journal of Communication* 23, 2: 160–8.

_____ (1980) 'Rules theories of communication: varieties, limitations and potentials', paper presented to the Speech Communication Association, New York.

Pike, K. L. (1966) 'Etic and emic standpoints for the description of behavior', in A. G. Smith (ed.) *Communication and Culture*, New York: Holt, Rinehart & Winston.

Reid, L. N. (1979) 'Viewing rules as mediating factors of children's responses to commercials', *Journal of Broadcasting* 23, 1: 15–26.

Sallach, D. L. (1974) 'Class domination and ideological hegemony', *Sociological Quarterly* 15, 1: 38–50.

Schiller, H. I. (1973) *The Mind Managers*, Boston: Beacon Press.

_____ (1976) *Communication and Cultural Domination*, White Plains, NY: International Arts and Sciences Press.

Shimanoff, S. (1980) *Communication Rules*, Beverly Hills, CA: Sage Publications.

Sigman, S. J. (1980) 'On communication rules from a social perspective', *Human Communication Research* 7, 1: 57–71.

Steiner, G. (1963) *The People Look at Television*, New York: Knopf.

Streicher, L. H. and Bonney, N. L. (1974) 'Children talk about television', *Journal of Communication* 24, 1: 54–61.

Toulmin, S. (1974) 'Rules and their relevance for understanding human behavior', in T. Mischel (ed.) *Understanding Other Persons*, Totowa, NJ: Rowan & Littlefield.

von Wright, G. H. (1962) 'Practical inference', *Philosophical Review* 22, 2: 159–79.

Wand, B. (1968) 'Television viewing and family choice differences', *Public Opinion Quarterly* 32, 1: 84–94.

Ward, S. and Wackman, D. B. (1973) 'Children's information processing of television advertisements', in P. Clarke (ed.) *New Models for Communication Research*, Beverly Hills, CA: Sage Publications.

Wartella, E. (1979) *Children Communicating: Media and Development of Thought, Speech, Understanding*, Beverly Hills, CA: Sage Publications.

5 How families select television programs: a mass-observational study

The experience of viewing television is embedded uniquely in on-going processes of family interaction, an empirical domain that is now receiving considerable attention by communication researchers. Recent ethnographic investigations have produced accounts which range from elaborate descriptions of a small number of family groups' contact with television to large-scale studies of the media habits of hundreds of families (Bryce 1980; Christol 1981; Lull 1976, 1980a; Melton, 1980). The latter methodological approach is sometimes known as 'mass observation' and derives from a tradition of family research that began in England during the 1930s and 1940s (Madge 1953). In the early British studies, numerous observers were trained to enter the homes of families in order to examine a standardized set of domestic activities.

The present study is a multi-method report that employs mass-observational and survey data that were gathered in order to examine one aspect of the construction of interpersonal activities involving television. Specifically, the study was designed to determine who is responsible for the selection of television programs at home, how program selection processes occur, and how the roles of family position and family communication patterns influence these activities.

Mass communication researchers have given some attention to the program selection process over the years. Niven found that a family decision is the means by which most families select programs at night, but that individuals control the set during the day (Niven 1960). He also reported that children were more likely than their parents to have their preferred programs viewed by the group. Smith found that housewives selected about 45 percent of the shows at night; general agreement decided 23 percent of the selections; husbands picked 23 percent of the shows; and children selected only 14 percent (Smith 1961). Smith also reported that families where the educational level of the parent(s) was high were more likely than other families to employ program selection by general agreement than by authoritarian control. He also concluded that 'housewives who are relatively unsophisticated are more often the selectors of television programs because television is more important to them' (Smith 1961: 43).

Wand (1968) found that Canadian families' program selection processes did not lead to 'family togetherness'. She found that mothers dominated fathers when they disagreed over what television show to watch, although fathers were generally perceived by family members as being in charge of the program selection process. In a naturalistic quasi-experiment, I also found that fathers were regarded by other family members as most influential in family discussions that were conducted in order to select shows via a 'family vote' process (Lull 1978). The findings also showed that fathers, mothers, and older children (13–18 years) were more likely than younger children to have their preferences selected for group viewing.

Viewing is often nonselective. Many audience members watch programs that simply happen to appear on the same channel to which the television is already tuned. Viewers often watch programs that are selected by someone else in the family. About three-fourths of the American population say that their daily viewing is characterized at least in part by these habits of nonselectivity (Comstock 1980). A focus group study undertaken by the Corporation for Public Broadcasting revealed that program selection decisions often are complicated interpersonal communication activities involving intrafamily status relations, temporal context, the number of sets available and rule-based communication conventions (Corporation for Public Broadcasting 1978).

The present study was designed to document family activities that involve control of the main television set. The primary data base resulted from mass observations of families. Program selection activities of families and related conceptual areas were also investigated with a postobservational survey. The findings produced by these methods in this relatively unexplored area are descriptive.

Using an elaboration of the indices employed in previous research, patterns of interpersonal communication characteristics of the families were also assessed and considered in relation to specific television-linked attitudes and activities (Lull 1980b). Family members answered questionnaire items designed to determine the degree to which they are 'concept-' or 'socio'-oriented. Concept-oriented families are those that value the presentation of personal points of view on issues under discussion and do not discourage disagreement or argumentation about these issues. Socio-oriented homes, on the other hand, are characterized by an environment where social harmony is prized and children are told to repress expression of ideas if it would cause interpersonal friction. Numerous studies have demonstrated that family communication patterns predict differential communications activity, including uses and effects of the mass media.

METHOD

The present research was designed systematically to focus the attention of nearly 100 observers on how families turn on, change channels and turn off the main television set in their homes. Undergraduate students from an upper division theoretical course in mass communication at a West Coast University were trained to observe the families who served as subjects for the study. Training of student observers involved participation in family simulation exercises as well as the observing and reporting of family communicative behavior which was viewed by the group on film. Personal contact was made with the families in the sample by the researchers prior to the observational period.

Observers spent most of two days with the families which were randomly assigned to them and returned a third day to conduct interviews with each family member. Families that took part in the study were members of the Goleta Valley Boys Club, a large, heterogeneous organization that exists in the vicinity of the University of California, Santa Barbara. In order to achieve the desired sample size, more than 500 families were contacted by telephone. Random procedures were used to develop the phone list and a high rate of rejection took place as it always does when this type of research is conducted (Lull 1985).

Observers spent two consecutive late afternoons and evenings with the families to which they were assigned. They ate dinner with the families and generally took part in all their activities. To the degree it was possible, families were asked to ignore the presence of the observer and carry out their routines in normal fashion. Previous data indicate that families' basic activities, including their television viewing, are not greatly disrupted by the presence of a trained observer. The observers took written notes in order to document as accurately as possible the activities that occurred. Since this study focused on the specific actions that surround the operation of the main television set, the observers were able to limit their observations and documentations to particular instances of interaction.

Families were not informed in advance that the intent of the observer was to examine television-related behavior. They were told that the observer was interested in studying 'family life' for a college class. Families watched television in great abundance during the observational sessions. Of the families that had a television set (all but two in the eventual sample), only one family failed to turn the set on at least once during the observational period.

Some 93 families were observed during the same week during late Autumn 1980. Of these groups, 74 were two-parent families. The one-parent families have been removed from the sample for this analysis. Most one-parent families had a woman as head of the household, and this condition could have systematically distorted an understanding of the role of fathers and mothers in the normative two-parent groups. This analysis then, considers 74 families comprised of 286 members. In total 74 fathers and 73 mothers were analyzed, the small discrepancy due to the failure of one of the mothers to complete a postobservational questionnaire. Child subjects numbered 139, comprising 48 percent of the sample.

Observers returned to the homes of the families with whom they stayed on a third day in order to interview each person. Family members were asked to report their perceptions of family position and communication patterns in their homes, to describe and evaluate the program selection processes in which they participate, to indicate the degree of selectivity employed in personal viewing, and to provide fundamental demographic information.

RESULTS

The primary issue – who is responsible for control of the main television set at home – is addressed by data presented in Tables 5.1 and 5.2. Responses to the postobservational questionnaire regarding personal influence in the choice of television programs are reported in Table 5.1. Fathers were named most often as the person or one of the persons who controls the selection of television programs (χ_2 = 30.93, $df = 6$, $p< 0.01$). Children and mothers were more likely to regard fathers this way than were the fathers themselves.

Table 5.1 Perceived dominant selectors of television programs[1]

Rater	Father	Mother	One child	Consensus	Parents	Children combination	Parent/child combination	Don't know
Father	19	24	8	14	15	10	4	7
Mother	29	16	12	15	6	14	3	6
Child	36	12	27	9	7	5	3	2
Total	30	16	18	12	8	8	3	5

1. Numbers in the table are percentages indicating how often each individual or combination of persons was designated as dominant by each rater. Slight row discrepancies are due to rounding error.

Table 5.2 Observed instances of control of main television set

Family position	Act alone	With discussion	Percent alone	Percent in family
Father	158	14	92	36
Mother	59	15	80	15
Child	136	11	93	30
Family consensus	4	23	15	6
Parents	7	6	54	3
Children combination	12	13	48	5
Parent/child combination	5	22	19	6
	381	104	79	101

Fathers believed that their mates were more responsible than any other single person or specific combination of individuals for determining the choice of programs. Overall, however, family members were just as likely to say that one of the children rather than the mother decides what is viewed on the main television set. Children often perceive themselves, or one of their siblings, as the primary controller of the set. Family consensus was another procedure that was mentioned. Particular combinations of parents and/or children were seldom regarded as the dominant modes for selection.

These perceptions were supported only in part by the observed instances of control of the main television set that were documented by the researchers who lived with the families. Observers noted who turned the set on, who changed the channel, and who turned the set off. They also documented whether or not these actions were undertaken with any discussion of what would be viewed. An act of control of the television set that was considered to have occurred 'alone' was when the person made the move without any conversation or simply announced his or her intention, such as 'Well, it's six o'clock and I'm going to watch the news'. Acts that were coded 'with discussion' involved sensitivity to the interests of other viewers or potential viewers in the conversation that accompanied the act. So, this portion of the analysis reveals who the controllers actually were and to what degree meaningful negotiation typified the interactions.

The observations indicate that fathers controlled more program decisions than any other single family member or combination of family viewers ($\chi_2 = 74.45$, $df=6$, $p< 0.01$, Table 5.2). They were more than twice as likely as their wives (or live-in female friends) to do so. Further, they acted alone in more than 90 percent of these decisions. One of the children was next most likely to turn the set on, turn it off or change the channel. Children were responsible for 30 percent of these actions (compared to 36 percent for their fathers) and they were also extremely likely to do so without discussion (93 percent of the time acting alone). Mothers were observed to be far less involved in the actual manipulation of the set than were either their husbands (or live-in male friends) or children. They were the initiators of only 15 percent of these actions. Further, they were less likely than either fathers or children to negotiate action alone. Still, they performed these acts without discussion 80 percent of the time. Other approaches to choosing programs, changing the channel, or turning off the set were sometimes used by families; however more than three-fourths of all set alterations were made by one family member. The vast majority of these actions were executed with no observable negotiation.

The influence of family position

Analyses of variance and Student-Newman-Keuls *post hoc* tests were conducted on a variety of dependent measures from the post-observational survey that concerned television program selection processes as they are influenced by family position (father, mother, child). Fathers did not differ from mothers on any of the measures. However, both parents differed from the children on several indices. Children said they were more likely than their parents to watch television programs that they did not select themselves ($F=6.31$, $df=2/283$, $p<0.01$). They were also more likely than mothers or fathers to watch 'television' instead of particular programs ($F=4.57$, $df=2/283$, $p<0.05$). Children were more likely than their parents to argue about what television shows to watch ($F=6.76$, $df=2/283$, $p<0.01$).

Further, children were less satisfied than their parents with the way their families made decisions, including the selection of television shows, and the outcomes of those decisions ($F=24.28$, $df=2/283$, $p<0.001$). Still, children were more likely than their parents to be satisfied with television as a form of family entertainment ($F=24.18$, $df=2/283$, $p<0.001$).

The influence of family communication patterns

Generally, family members who perceived their communication at home to be concept-oriented were more likely than members of socio-oriented homes to have distinctive activities and attitudes that involve the use of television (Table 5.3). First, amount of viewing was negatively associated with concept orientation and uncorrelated with socio orientation. A measure of satisfaction with the family's selection of television programs was uncorrelated with summed concept and summed socio orientation scores. However, sensitivity to others in the program selection process was positively associated

Table 5.3 Correlations of selected family activities with family communication

Questionnaire item	Summed concept scores	Summed socio scores
How satisfied are you with your family's selection of television programs in general?	0.07	−0.08
How satisfied are you that other family members care about what you want to see on television?	0.13*	−0.11*
How often do you watch television programs that you haven't selected yourself?	−0.13*	0.07
How often do you watch 'television' instead of particular shows?	−0.12*	0.06
How satisfied are you with television as a form of family entertainment?	−0.21**	0.08
How often do you argue with other family members about what television shows to watch?	−0.03	0.11*
How satisfied are you with the ways your family makes decisions about things in general?	0.28**	0.03
Amount of television viewed per day	−0.21**	0.08

Note: Entries are Pearson product-moment zero-order correlations. One asterisk indicates that significance was reached at 0.05; two asterisks indicate significance at 0.01.

with concept orientation and negatively associated with socio orientation.

Selective viewing was more typical of concept-oriented families than it was of socio-oriented groups. Concept orientation was negatively associated with watching programs that were not selected by the individual or watching 'television' instead of particular shows. Socio orientation was uncorrelated with both of these indices. Further, concept orientation correlated negatively with satisfaction with television as a form of family entertainment. Socio orientation was positively associated with the frequency of argumentation that accompanies the selection of television programs while concept orientation scores were not correlated with arguing. Finally, concept orientation was strongly related to satisfaction with the ways decisions are made in the home.

DISCUSSION

This study was conducted in order to document at first hand the ways in which two-parent families choose television programs. Observed activities ranged from one family which never communicated verbally about programs they wanted to watch, to another family which employed a loud charismatic prayer ritual each night so that 'God can tell us what shows to watch'. Observational and survey data have been presented in order to outline the fundamental character of some specific television-related interpersonal activities.

The locus of control in the program selection process can be explained primarily by family position. Family communication patterns were employed successfully as a predictor concept which also helped explain variability in the attitudes and activities of family members regarding the program selection process and the regulative interpersonal behaviors that underlie these actions.

The literature on family television program selection activities was unclear about who controls the set. In this study, observational and survey data converged to convincingly demonstrate that fathers had more perceived and actual control of the selection of television programs than any other individual in the family. Mothers were the least influential family member in this regard. About three-fourths of all program selections were made by one person and took place with little or no discussion or negotiation. Routines for viewing, even those operating during the first few weeks of the television season, occurred in a rule-governed, routinized fashion that apparently required little conversation in most homes.

While mothers and fathers were observed to differ in their program selection behavior, and were perceived by each other to differ in this activity, they did not differ in other aspects of viewing. Fathers and mothers reported the same amount of selectivity in viewing, argumentation over program choice, and satisfaction with family decision-making processes. However, both parents differed from children in these areas. Therefore, fundamental differences in several important aspects of the television viewing experience emerged when parents were compared to children. Children were less selective viewers, less happy with family decision-making processes, yet happier with television in general.

The type of family communication that takes place at home is significantly related to attitudes toward television. Not surprisingly, concept-oriented family members view less television, do so more selectively, and are less satisfied with television as a form of family entertainment. However, concept-oriented individuals were also more likely than those with a socio orientation to report that sensitivity to the needs of others exists in their interpersonal interaction about program selection. Further, socio-oriented family members said that arguments about programs prevailed more often in their homes than did people from concept-oriented households. These differences were not explained by a difference in the number of television sets which occupy concept and socio homes since no statistical relationship was found between number of sets and family communication type. The interesting conclusion, then, is that members of socio-oriented homes are *less* sensitive to the needs of others and more argumentative when television programs are selected than are individuals from the less harmonious concept-oriented homes.

In summary, the choosing and viewing of television programs, among our culture's most commonly practiced activities, are intricate family routines that have not yet been studied in depth by communication researchers. This study combined extensive observational data with survey data in order to approach an understanding of one aspect of how families construct time spent with television. Family roles and communication patterns were each found to influence exposure to television. Hopefully, the quantified mass observations and survey data presented here will help stimulate additional analyses of the interpersonal aspects of our society's immoderate involvement with television.

This chapter was originally published in *Journal of Broadcasting*, 26, 4, 1982.

REFERENCES

Bryce, J. (1980) 'Living with television: an exploratory ethnographic study of families and television', doctoral dissertation, Columbia University.

Christol, S. (1981) 'An ethnographic investigation of Mexican families' socialization to American television', paper presented to the Conference on Culture and Communication, Philadelphia.

Comstock, G. (1980) *Television in America*, Beverly Hills, CA: Sage Publications.

Corporation for Public Broadcasting (1978) *A Qualitative Study: The Effect of Television on People's Lives*, Washington, DC: CPB Office of Communication Research.

Lull, J. (1976) 'Mass media and family communication: an ethnography of audience behavior', doctoral dissertation, University of Wisconsin-Madison.

_____ (1978) 'Choosing television programs by family vote', *Communication Quarterly* 26, 1: 53–7.

_____ (1980a) 'The social uses of television', *Human Communication Research* 6, 3: 197–209.

_____ (1980b) 'Family communication patterns and the social uses of television', *Communication Research* 7, 3: 319–34.

_____ (1985) 'Ethnographic studies of broadcast media audiences', in J. Dominick and J. Fletcher (eds) *Broadcasting Research Methods*, Boston: Allyn & Bacon.

Madge, J. (1953) *The Tools of Social Science*, London: Longmans, Green.

Melton, R. (1980) 'Topic shift, topical agenda, and eye-gaze behavior in the presence of television', paper presented to the Western Speech Communication Association, Portland, OR.

Niven, H. (1960) 'Who in the family selects the TV program?', *Journalism Quarterly* 37, 1: 110–11.

Smith, D. C. (1961) 'The selectors of television programs', *Journal of Broadcasting* 6, 1: 35–44.

Wand, B. (1968) 'Television viewing and family choice differences', *Public Opinion Quarterly* 32, 1: 84–94.

6 China's *New Star*: the reformation on prime-time television

No television program produced in China has ever created a reaction among viewers to match the response given to the political drama *New Star* (*Xin Xing*, pronounced 'shin shin'), a twelve-part series which was telecast on the national network a few months prior to our arrival there in 1986. We had no knowledge of this program beforehand, but its importance became apparent to us very early during our interviewing. By the time we had talked with half a dozen families in Shanghai, our first research site, the name of the program had been mentioned spontaneously so often that we knew we had to explore the significance of the controversial show in detail. We added two simple questions to our list of open-ended inquiries that were asked of all families: 'Did you watch the drama series *New Star*? What did you think of it?'

From these questions families often launched into lengthy and sometimes very emotional descriptions of not only the program, but the sensitive political issues that are taken up in the show – the current reformation effort in China (*gai ge*), and specifically, a questioning of the competence of the country's middle-level bureaucrats – the managers, officials, cadre – known in Chinese as the *ganbu*. Family members spoke freely about these matters, an openness that likely was enhanced by the fact that we had inquired about a television show and had not asked for their opinions about political issues directly. While Chinese citizens in the cities spoke (even critically) without fear of reprisal, I believe that their remarks about conditions of work, for instance, were far more freely forthcoming when placed in the context of the themes and storylines of a hugely popular television program. This was a fortunate methodological circumstance that permits analysis of this show not only in terms of its artistic quality and appeal, but also in light of some of

China's most pressing social and political issues – themes that were embodied passionately in the program itself.

By presenting *New Star* on the national network, Chinese television achieved a degree of relevance that, for one thing, promoted the medium as an instrument not only of entertainment and information, but of hope for the creation of a better society. The program aired during a period of great public support for Deng Xiaoping, his last years in official command of the Communist Party. The themes taken up in the story, and the very appearance of the program on television, reflect the major political currents in China in 1986 – the reformist pragmatism of Deng standing in historical contrast to the ideological puritanism of Mao Zedong. *New Star* will be remembered as one symbol of the Deng era in China, especially the decade of such great optimism following the Cultural Revolution, culminating in the late 1980s when, by means of television, virtually all urban homes, and many in the countryside as well, had simultaneous access to the same story – a development that is without precedent in China. *New Star* is a piece of electronic literature that touched nearly everyone.

As we shall see, the drama of *New Star* turns on the encounters of a fictional young communist political and economic reformer – the 'new star' – Li Xianlan (pronounced 'Lee Shan-lan'). Li's heroism stems from his courage to implement effective reforms in the face of stiff resistance from China's conservative old guard. There is virtually no violence in *New Star*. Li is a warrior against the muddled Chinese bureaucracy, its history of inefficiency, unfairness, and reputation for placing profound constraints on the development of human potential. The program was popular mainly because the story resonated so well with the conditions and frustrations that workers and peasants routinely experience in their own lives. The production format also fit the story. *New Star* was a political soap opera, replete with intricate interpersonal status relations, a love triangle, family intertwinings, and traumas and tragedies of unbelievable proportions. The constant use of close-up and extreme close-up shots of the actors and actresses created an intensely personal feeling to the show that enhanced its emotionally charged political significance and impact. The contemporary reformation in China is a kind of soap opera in real life. Television's treatment of the story within the formulaic conventions of the melodrama was appropriate and compelling.

China's famed plan for modernization has caught the attention of governments, international corporations, journalists, and scholars throughout the world. *New Star* is a story about the modernization too, but it does *not* focus solely on technological and economic reform. The program is a blunt criticism of the heavy bureaucraticism that has plagued China throughout its history and the social consequences that it brings. At one level *New Star* appears to be a kind of introspective attack on the current management dilemma in China – an exposé of the widespread incompetence and abuse perpetrated by many *ganbu* that has discouraged millions of young Chinese workers, who are intimidated by their bosses in a system that rarely allows for the willful changing of jobs. At the same time, *New Star* represents the 'new feeling' in China, in the words of one of our narrators, the spirit and consensus of the people who, throughout history, have been undaunted in their nationalistic optimism generally and in their irrepressive certainty that China is forever on the 'threshold of a new day' that promises finally to fulfill the great destiny of the country (Pye 1985: 182).

So, *New Star* is a story about two fundamental and seemingly contradictory issues – the potential progress that is promised by the reformation and the haunting obstacle of the punishing bureaucracy that is so steadfastly in place, personified by the old *ganbu*. Unlike the often sensationalistic accounts of the modernization that appear in the foreign press, this is a story about the *internal* dynamics of the modernization that was written by a Chinese man, appeared on the Chinese national television system (and many regional outlets in addition), was viewed, at least in part, by nearly everyone in the country, and stimulated an enthusiastic reaction by viewers. A major achievement of the program, from the point of view of the progressive forces in China at least, is that the very appearance of *New Star* on the nation's television system gave credence to public complaints about the *ganbu* problem while it cast an image of the possibility of a radically new style of party leadership.

The story of *New Star* is also an account of the power of television, the great storyteller of our time, radiating its influence throughout a society. I shall tell the story of *New Star* from several perspectives – the producer, the originating broadcast station, the network, researchers, and most important, the audience members. The analysis includes many verbatim descriptions and opinions that were expressed by the viewers of *New Star*.

THE CHINESE REFORMATION: CAN IT REALLY HAPPEN?

'During the Cultural Revolution the government told us, "you are good, you are good". But we were hungry. Why did they say we were good when we were hungry?' (42-year-old battery salesman from Beijing)

'Look at my body. I am healthy. Deng took control and now we have a higher standard of living. You can eat whatever you want. In the past even peanuts were rationed by the government. Now nobody likes to eat peanuts.' (33-year old male worker in a Shanghai boat factory)

Improvements that have taken place in China since the end of the Cultural Revolution are widely recognized by the people. The increase in national production and the improvement of the living standard, including wide ownership of television sets, are among the most visible indications of success in the post-Mao era. At the same time, most Chinese citizens believe that a restructuring of many political and social aspects of Chinese society is still necessary in order to advance not only China's internal and external economic position, but to develop further the human potential of its massive population. This task is made most difficult today because of the immense bureaucracy (that had grown to include more than 75 million cadre under Mao) that penetrates all aspects of life in China. The reformation requires repair of the inefficient and often corrupt management practices that penetrate so many dimensions of the ubiquitous public sphere:

'It's not that we are dissatisfied with the Communist Party, we just need to take the true advantage of socialism and apply it to our real life. Even Deng Xiaoping says that the style of the party must change. They have had this disease (bureaucratism) for a long time.' (45-year-old male furniture factory worker, Beijing)

'The idea of the reformation is well matched with young people now.' (16-year-old female radio factory worker, Xian)

'In my office everybody thinks that China needs to be reformed. Young people especially think it's very important.' (22-year-old male hospital administration clerk, Beijing)

'Now everybody realizes that we need to reform. But it's hard to walk a step ahead in my own job, so I can imagine how difficult it is to accomplish the reformation. Still, with no change, there is no future for China.' (49-year-old male English teacher at a business college, Xian)

'To "think" the reformation is much easier than to "do" it. We haven't done it.' (28-year-old taxi driver, Guangzhou)

Under Deng, the government forthrightly recognized the problem of China's unmanageable management system, the human penalties it imposes on peasants and workers, and the need for a political reform that embraces changes in management procedures at the work-unit level. Deng himself outlined the problem in 1980:

> Bureaucratism is expressed in sitting high above the people, using power in an indiscriminate way, becoming divorced from reality and the masses, being fond of keeping up appearances, a liking for uttering empty words, mental ossification, sticking to old ways and conventions, swollen bureaucracy, delaying the handling of matters, paying no attention to inefficiency, failing to take responsibility, failing to keep one's word, endless circulation of official documents, and mutual passing of the buck. All this results in a stuffy atmosphere, reprimanding others on the slightest provocation, retaliating against people, suppressing democracy, cheating those above and hoodwinking those below, acting in an imperious and despotic way, engaging in bribery and corruption, and so on . . . all this has reached an intolerable stage. (Nathan 1985: 75)

These formidable problems are exacerbated by China's history of a lack of a legal system or clear and sustaining policy, contradictions that exist between prescribed ideological positions and actual practices that occur in everyday life (especially at work), constant rumors in the late 1980s about Deng's health, the uncertainty that surrounds China's process of political succession, speculations about the ideological leanings of the array of various leaders who have emerged since Deng's resignation, and the ideological equivocations of national agencies of information and socialization, particularly the official press.

None the less, there are indications of change within the system of governance in China that have promoted optimism among the people. A constitutional revision written in 1982 strengthened the power of law over idiosyncratic decisions proclaimed by party officials in several areas of public life. The 'responsibility system' was successfully introduced in farming and factory production, at once providing incentives to workers and gradually reducing the authority of many *ganbu*. The government admitted that workers' initiative and quality of life had been 'dampened' by the rigid egalitarianism of the previous decades, and a need for change was necessary since 'production [had been] hindered' (*China Facts and Figures* 1986). Communes were out, collectives were in, each operating under a contract system that was designed formally to describe rights and responsibilities in economic relations between workers and bosses. Doctors and other professionals are sometimes now required to sign contracts for work, then meet the requirements or face possible replacement. Officials have begun to undergo 'evaluation sessions' in some cities where workers are free to voice their criticisms 'in an effort to get rid of bureaucracy and promote office democracy', according to *China Daily*. The power and privileges of many ranking party officials appeared to be on the decline by 1990, and proposals to separate government functions from the Communist Party were recommended as 'urgent and necessary', according to Xinhua, the government news service.

RESISTANCE TO THE REFORMATION: *GANBU* IN SERVICE OF THE STATUS QUO AND THE *GUANXI* PROBLEM

'China is not like other countries where you can make money or be famous because of your talent. Here the relationships make it much more complicated.' (19-year-old male art school student, and son of parents who are party members, Beijing)

'I work with no opinion.' (29-year-old female worker in a video cassette recorder factory, Shanghai)

The impact of China's concrete achievements and the excitement that is promised for the future is confounded and diffused by the day-to-day experiences of the vast majority of urban workers. They made it clear to us that improvements promised by reformers in Beijing have not yet filtered into the workplaces they occupy. I want to illustrate substantively the depth of this problem by recounting actual conditions of work that were described in detail by our narrators.

A key feature of the problem is the practice of *guanxi* (pronounced 'gwan shee'), a form of interpersonal relations in China based on the reciprocal giving of favors. The practice is consistent with the Chinese habit of family members and friends 'taking care of each other'. *Guanxi* is an informally institutionalized 'I'll scratch your back if you'll scratch mine' way of doing business that, while officially discouraged, is widely practiced. *Guanxi* derives from the Chinese concept of *bao*, or 'social investments', where the giving of a favor carries an unspoken, but firmly recognized expectation that the 'giver' expects to receive a favor of equal weight in return (see especially Gold 1985 for a detailed discussion of this communications practice). One builds *guanxi*. A person has 'good' *guanxi* with somebody else. *Guanxi* is a purely pragmatic strategy. Economic scarcity and a system that provides limited opportunities for individuals to promote their own interests through official channels breed dependence on personal connections – *guanxi*. The potential for exercising the practice of *guanxi* is not evenly distributed within the population. People who supervise official functions (for example those who assign housing, promote workers, permit marriages, or admit students to universities) are in positions to require favors in return.

These *guanxi* relationships can easily promote the bureaucratism that is criticized by Deng. And while the government in China seems to have sincerely attempted to discourage *guanxi*, it still exists even at the highest levels in China. According to an account published by Reuters news service in 1987, Hu Yaobang, the late Communist Party leader and leading reformer who had opposed China's 'old boy network' (*lao-haoren*), created in large measure through the practice of *guanxi*, lost power when he refused to appoint the offspring of some elderly Central Committee members to high positions in government. For workers and peasants the interpersonal networks and the system of favor-giving that holds them together is a routine feature of everyday life:

> 'There is no way to close the back door. You even need a relationship with a store clerk to get what you want [when items are scarce]. It's not fair.' (26-year-old female travel agent for river tours, Shanghai)

Guanxi as a means for development of pragmatic interdependencies is but part of the sensitive issue of interpersonal relationships in China, most evident in the work setting. Workers are really at the mercy of their *ganbu* – the middle-level managers of China's factories, farms, offices, and agencies. Many workers see their *ganbu* as members of a different social class – a privileged class. This is not a recent phenomenon. Cadre and worker positions were very different during the Mao era too, despite the egalitarian rhetoric of the time (Dietrich 1986: 278).

There are many problems inherent in the worker–*ganbu* relationship, beginning with the fact that many managers are not respected much by their workers. The difficulty begins with a questioning of the qualifications and competencies of the *ganbu*:

'My work unit leader is a party member and a Viet Nam veteran. He got a special government award and was given a leadership position because of it. Otherwise there is no special quality to this man. He is of terrible ability. He cannot control production.' (28-year-old male worker in an automobile factory, Shanghai)

'The old *ganbu* are too conservative. They miss the contemporary way of thinking and they have no guts. They "look left and look right". They create problems for young people and that is our society's problem.' (22-year-old male hotel employee, Beijing)

'Middle-level *ganbu* are very conservative and stubborn. This is because they never had a chance to see how fast the world is developing. They only think, "we are so good". They are narrow-minded. They say, "follow me", but no one is willing to take responsibility.' (63-year-old male school administrator, Shanghai)

The negative stereotype of China's middle-level managers is that they are inefficient, lacking in ideological vision, poorly educated, old, abusive, corrupt, jealous of young workers, vindictive, protective of their private interests (in traditional China and even now in the modern era it is considered a disgrace to flaunt one's private interests) and often gained their positions through political favoritism – hardly the right type of leader in the era of modernization. They reward the 'yes' man and woman and punish troublemakers – people who disagree with them. Workers' rights are few, and there is no effective system for fair redress of grievances in any case. As a result, many workers fear their bosses and develop strategies for coping and not standing out:

'I don't work too hard. If you are a good worker the *ganbu* won't give you a day off. So, I just fool around and pass the time at work.' (26-year-old male factory worker, Shanghai)

'They give you a job and you just work the job. We are not naughty . . . we don't fool around or make trouble. We come to work on time and we don't leave too early. We just try to blend in.' (32-year-old female electronic assembly worker, Beijing)

'Generally the attitude at work is, "you don't bother me and I won't bother you".' (33-year-old male factory worker, Shanghai)

'In our daily life when we find a problem with our *ganbu* nobody wants to say anything. Everybody is afraid to wear the small shoes (to be eternally punished). So we don't always see the problems of our *ganbu*. We open one eye, but we close the other eye.' (30-year-old female accountant in an electronic products retail store, Shanghai)

'When we think about why someone in our department is *shien jing* (considered to be outstanding: literally, "first, keep going") usually it is because of his relationship ability.' (49-year-old accountant for a redistributable products company, Shanghai)

'If you have a good relationship with the *ganbu* you don't have to work very hard. Even good workers who don't have a good relationship will never have a chance to be *shien jing*. In your whole life you just work.' (26-year-old female television factory worker, Shanghai. She is the daughter of the woman who made the comment quoted directly above)

Listening to so many Chinese people describe this atmosphere at work reminds me of life in the military. Low and middle-ranking officers rise to their institutionalized level of incompetence where, in a system of highly structured statuses and a constant threat of punishment, they unleash their authority in a way that rewards mindless compliance and discriminates against progress. In many Chinese work units, as in the military, the supreme value is conformity. This can be carried to visible extremes. In some work units (*danwei*) it is enough to simply show up at work and not bother anybody. I watched several waitresses and bus boys sleep through a meeting of restaurant workers led by their *ganbu* in Shanghai. Workers in offices throughout the country routinely read newspapers and books and do other things while they are at their desks, even while their bosses are close by. So long as they finish their assigned work and don't disturb workplace harmony, they are free to do as they please. Clerks in many stores ignore their customers and only carry out the most basic duty by staying at their work stations until it is time to go home.

Another problem frequently reported concerns the higher education and specialized training of ambitious and bright workers. Many *ganbu* don't want these workers to study abroad, for instance, because the student-workers often have high unofficial status when they return to China, an automatic credibility that makes some *ganbu* jealous. There is a Chinese expression, 'to keep someone short', meaning that people in power who are jealous of 'taller' people (meaning smarter, better educated, or more clever) and will find ways to limit the taller one's potential. This is one reason why so many Chinese who study overseas do not want to return to China. Lucien Pye has described this problem and recounts an interesting story:

> Even more troubling are the reports that students trained abroad in technical skills appropriate for China's modernizing effort are not effectively used when they return to China. The problem does not lie with the top leadership, who apparently want to upgrade the Chinese pool of modern trained talent, [but with] [l]ocal cadres, who have less education, may be resentful and may exploit China's egalitarian system by making petty demands on the returned students. In a particularly noteworthy, but not untypical case, Xiu Ruijuan achieved the remarkable distinction while at Stanford of publishing her research, which became known in medical literature as the Xiu Theory; but upon getting back to China she was assigned to the modest position of 'deputy research fellow' in her medical institute until the scandal came to the attention of Hu Yaobang, after which she was made a research assistant. (Pye 1985: 194)

Obviously I have painted a very bad picture of China's middle-level bureaucrats. But the themes outlined so far were repeated over and over by Chinese family members. Of course, some favorable reports were given by workers about their bosses. Several people spoke proudly of the accomplishments of their work-units, the talents of the *ganbu* there, and the hope this offers Chinese society. Typically, however, favorable accounts were given about young or well-educated *ganbu*. Many management positions in China's cities now require high or specialized education.

Eradicating or, more realistically, reducing the *ganbu* problem cannot help but be an extremely slow process, regardless of high-level intentions and instructions. Many cadre consider the reformation to be a threat. They fear a loss of power and possibly the loss of their jobs. Most *ganbu* believe that they deserve to hold their positions. They won those jobs through a contribution of some sort – often through sheer loyalty to the old system. They are hard-nosed 'old boys' (most are men) who cannot be moved out easily. Regardless of how they got their jobs (political maneuvering during the Cultural Revolution is an often-mentioned and hated reason), it seems impossible to deconstruct the structure in which they are embedded, regardless of ideological pronouncements. The Communist Party, then, is stuck in part with the image of the incompetent *ganbu*. Many people admitted that ultimately the best hope for reform is to simply wait for better qualified men and women of the next generation to take over these leadership positions. Indeed, this has already begun.

THE REFORMATION WILL BE TELEVISED

'. . . I think that most people want reformation. We need to reform, otherwise we cannot be a strong and rich country . . . (*New Star*) . . . really shows how the old *ganbu* cannot follow the new thinking . . . (also) *New Star* reflects people's problems and criticisms. This is the main reason why we put *New Star* on the air.' (Wang Chuan Yu, Chief Editor, CCTV, Beijing)

'. . . without reformation we cannot continue to move our country forward. So, this is the most popular current issue among audience members. *New Star* just matches the tendency that everybody is talking about – the reformation.' (Pan Huiming, Deputy Director, Guandong Province Television Station, Guangzhou)

The world's largest television audience watched a fictionalized version of the reformation unfold in their homes when *New Star* was telecast in China. The appearance and appeal of the young reformer – Li Xianlan – and the bold critique of the bureaucracy and bureaucrats was most timely. Li became television's version of the vigorous leader who is expected to lead China in the spirit of the Gengshen reforms of 1980 and subsequent plans for national modernization. The setting for the story, rural China, was appropriate since early reformation efforts were directed toward revamping the concept of communal labor in the countryside in hopes for minimizing bureaucratic sluggishness and increasing agricultural production. While the Cultural Revolution had legitimized and strengthened the bureaucratic structure that still dominates the country today, *New Star* is a feature *sui generis* of a new Cultural Revolution, a struggle to revamp some of China's most deeply entrenched social and political practices.

DEVELOPMENT OF THE TELEVISION SERIES

Ironically, in a national system that is based so fundamentally on planning, the most important television program ever produced in the country found its way onto the air via an irregular and controversial path. *New Star* was not designed originally to be a television program and it was broadcast on the national network almost by accident. The popularization of *New Star* is itself a fascinating story.

The story on which the television series was based was written by Kuo Yun Lu, a factory employee who lives in Shanxi Province, a dry and dusty expanse of land located in the northeast part of the country. The author is a member of that generation of Chinese men and women whose most formative years were interrupted by the Cultural Revolution. Kuo was dispatched to the countryside in 1968 before he had reached 20 years of age. That experience, combined with his extreme interest in the structure of leadership in China and his contact with persons in power who were sympathetic to his viewpoint, inspired him to begin writing a story about the carrying out of China's reformation. The result was a novel, *New Star*.

The novel was first published in 1984 as a series of articles in a literary magazine (*Contemporary*) and was also produced as a radio soap opera, but neither the articles nor the radio broadcasts received much attention from the public. In late 1984, however, a new television station operating in Shanxi Province began to transmit programs for the first time. Operating out of an old building with little equipment and only 1,000 watts of radiating power, the station broadcasts from the city of Taiyuan, located in the middle of the province, about 200 miles southwest of Beijing. Programmers at Taiyuan Television (TYTV) had little experience developing locally originating programs but *New Star* seemed to be an excellent candidate since the author is from the area and the story had already been written. The station's only previous attempt to air an original drama (*Jin Ein Wan*, a story about the life of a miner) was criticized as 'too plain' and had not attracted much of an audience. Fully aware of the sensitive nature of the story in *New Star*, the managers of TYTV decided to produce the novel in the form of a television docudrama mini-series. While it can be reasonably argued in retrospect that the story actually promotes a perspective on the reformation advocated by the contemporary Communist Party, this interpretation was certainly far less clear to the authorities at TYTV at the time. Their decision to produce and air this program – the

Photo 6.1: The logo for the tiny regional television station in Shanxi Province (Taiyuan TV), originator of China's most important television program, appears at the beginning of each episode of *New Star*.

first ever about the reformation, and by far the most critical television show ever produced in China – was a courageous act. *New Star* was not a drama based on distant history. The controversies and problems that were presented are not fictional.

There was not much money or equipment available to produce the twelve hour-long episodes. In the end, the program was produced for about 250,000 yuan – the equivalent of about $800,000 US, about half of what it would have cost to produce *one* feature-length film in China at that time. Still, the series came in under budget by 50,000 yuan. Originally the production company had only one box of stage property and a single camera that was borrowed from the Taiyuan Iron and Steel Company. Station personnel and the producer of the program – Ching Dar Li – admit that the challenge they faced in producing *New Star* was a sobering one at the beginning. The station was a 'start-up' operation and financial resources were slim. But excitement and a positive spirit surrounded the production of *New Star* from the very beginning.

High-ranking government authorities in Taiyuan agreed with the perspective on the reformation that is portrayed in the story. They enthusiastically endorsed the series and raised more than 300,000 yuan in support of the production and promised more money if needed. Volunteers were everywhere. The province police department donated uniformed guards and a doctor to work on the shooting location. When 'extras' were needed on the set, these uniformed workers changed into farmworkers' clothes and became part of the production. In order to keep costs down, virtually everyone associated with the production, including the producer, director, stage manager, even the stage hands, also had roles in the story. Hundreds of local villagers and farmers also volunteered to assist in the production and were dumbfounded when the production company tried to pay them for their services. To the very end, the 'extras' refused to accept money for their parts in the production.

Everyone involved in the production – including the producer, director, and the main actors and actresses – were part of the spirit behind the production of *New Star*. They had a sense that what they were doing was not only important artistically, but politically as well. No one on the set demanded any special privileges or treatment. The emphasis was on efficiency – produce the show within budget and do it quickly. Everyone arrived on the set early each day, ate their meals there, and many of them slept on location – even when the shooting was done in remote mountainous areas.

New Star was directed by Lee Shin, a little-known director from the talent pool of the Beijing Film Production Company. He made the decisions about who would be given the major roles and he carefully selected actors and actresses who were not particularly well known but who were caught up in the spirit of the project – both the ideological nuances of the story and the idea of helping to establish a new and important television station. When the production contract for *New Star* was first negotiated, two other companies (Chang Cheng Film Production Company and the Chinese TV Drama Production Center) also came to Shanxi Province to compete for the right to produce the show. But officials from TYTV settled on the small production unit whose leaders had so aggressively pursued the project and refused to be intimidated by the presence of the larger production companies during the negotiations.

The twelve episodes of *New Star* were produced in 102 days, averaging less than nine days' shooting time per installment, a remarkable achievement given the variety of locations and number of actors involved. The series was first broadcast on the local province station, TYTV, beginning on the first anniversary of the new station. Audience response far surpassed expectations, attracting the attention of the entire city. Based on its overwhelming success at TYTV, *New Star* was 'bicycled' to dozens of other local stations in China where it also became very popular.

The producer, Ching Dar Li, and the others from the production team would not be satisfied, however, until *New Star* had a national audience. They wanted the show to be distributed throughout China on the national television network, CCTV, and tried to convince the broadcasting officials in Beijing to put it on the air. There was no serious question in Beijing about the overall quality of the program or its ability to attract an audience large enough to justify presentation on the national network. However, there was concern about the sensitive political content of the drama. Never in China's history had a program with such direct criticism been telecast. Despite the potential difficulties, CCTV broadcast the series in winter and early spring, 1986.

The decision-making process that led to airing *New Star* on the network remains something of a mystery. As the story has been told to me, the series was received and supported by a ranking network official who was only filling the position temporarily. There remains even today a question as to whether or not the highest level officials at the network ever previewed and approved the program. Still, at least one meeting was held about *New Star* after which approval to air the show was granted. Precedence was extremely important. The series had already been presented on many city and province stations throughout China. Had the program not been aired by other stations, or if it had been aired only by TYTV and rejected by other province stations, it is unlikely that the network would have touched it. The fact that there are few high-quality drama series produced in China also helped *New Star* find a network slot. Television is a medium with a voracious appetite. It was an attractive proposition for the network to carry a show that had already been produced.

Circumstances surrounding the way *New Star* was produced further enhanced its chances for being aired on CCTV. Content of the original novel and the shooting of the series in Shanxi province was not under serious scrutiny by censors. There was little chance for interference or termination of the project during the making of the show. *New Star* arrived at CCTV as a finished product. While a film can be evaluated in one sitting by government officials, a twelve-part television series is far more cumbersome to review. Some Chinese scholars have speculated that had *New Star* been a film instead of a television series, it would not have passed the censors or would have been toned down.

Despite all the mysteries and complications, a decision was reached to put *New Star* on the air at CCTV and to place it during peak viewing time in the evenings. *New Star* appeared on CCTV during the dead of winter when family members are most likely to be inside their homes at night – watching television.

The national exposure thrilled people in Taiyuan. According to one account published in China, when the familiar theme song from the show pierced the airwaves and the TYTV logo appeared on the CCTV channel in Taiyuan, the local television contingent excitedly ran outside its offices and ignited a firecracker to celebrate its appearance on the Network (Wu 1986).

Additional meetings about *New Star* were held at the network offices in Beijing *after* the first two episodes were broadcast. The program had created a national controversy soon after the first segments appeared. While feedback from audiences throughout the country was overwhelmingly positive, high-ranking government officials were divided in their view of the appropriateness of the program. Some were adamantly opposed to it. Clearly, a decision to pull the program off the air would have been extremely damaging to the Chinese government which was promoting the idea of the national reformation at the time. *New Star* had become at once an extremely popular show (although there are no audience ratings taken so the actual size of the audience will never be known), a topic of conversation throughout the country, and a public relations problem for a government that was trying to display a more open and self-critical attitude. A new decision was reached to allow the series to continue. This decision seems to have been the right one, according to officials with whom we talked. Interestingly, one family member with whom we spoke said that one of *New Star*'s best effects was to influence China's high-level leaders who he reasoned were as likely as anyone else to be watching.

'NEW STAR FEVER'

Reaction to *New Star* on the network came from all directions. Most of it was favorable. Audience members spontaneously sent an unprecedented number of letters to the network praising the broadcasters for airing a program of such great relevance. The stunning response to *New Star* motivated one Chinese sociologist, Zhou Yong-ping, to conduct a large-scale audience survey about the program. He labeled the phenomenon, '*New Star* fever':

The people endured the whole winter sluggishly, and now they wake up from the sound of thunder (*New Star*) . . . When we are awakened . . . we cannot stop thinking why *New Star* can have such a huge influence, from children to old people, from the masses to the *ganbu*, from the workers to the professionals, the professors, and the intellectuals . . . In our memory, it seems that not any literary or artistic production has had such deep influence and popular appeal. (Zhou 1986: p. 1)

The program was a critical success. Newspapers paid much attention to the show. Critics awarded the program the 'Golden Eagle' award and the 'Sky Flying' award for excellence in a drama series. When the lead actors were not nominated for individual awards, the oversight became a minor scandal in the country, eventually causing a strain in the relationship between the production group and the actors. A juicy piece of gossip was that some production executives believed that the show had succeeded in spite of the performances of the lead actors, and that they were purposefully not nominated for the individual awards, an account that is denied by the producer. While the program was criticized softly by network officials who claimed that the artistic and production level of the program was not high (attributed to the 'lack of experience' at TYTV) and was faulted by some audience members (to be explored below), the consensus was clear: *New Star* was a television series of unmatched importance.

Television was not only the political agenda setter but also the popularizer of the story. The success of the television series led to publication of *New Star* as a book that has sold out several printings and is still in demand. Part of the popularity of the book is related to the lack of video cassette recorders and video tapes in China which would permit recording and repeated viewing of the show. The way to preserve the story is with the novel.

NEW STAR – A STORY OF THE CHINESE REFORMATION

The television series has many characteristics of Chinese literature. The story is complex and slow developing, full of double meanings and innuendoes. In the following paragraphs, I will outline the basic storyline, episode by episode, in order to reveal its major themes and to provide interpretations of the cultural and political subtleties that are woven into the program.[1]

The drama hinges most basically on an ideological conflict

between the two main characters – Li Xianlan and Gu Rong – and the intricate relationship between their families. This meshing of social histories and political circumstances, embedded and embroiled in the controversies that surround China's reformation, is part of what made *New Star* so popular. It is exactly this atmosphere of personal interdependencies and politics that so many Chinese people complain about. Several subplots and stories – not just political struggles, but family traumas and love affairs too – emerged throughout the series. But the core of the story, and the theme that was discussed by audiences everywhere in China, is the conflict between the handsome young political reformer, Li, and the guardian of the status quo, the old *ganbu*, Gu.

I will now describe in greatly abbreviated form what happens in each episode. The main characters, story developments, and the most important underlying implications will be introduced along the way. The two main characters, Li and Gu, will be referred to by their family names only. Others who have the same family name, Gu Shaoli and Gu Heng, for instance, will be called by their generational/personal names (e.g. 'Shaoli' and 'Heng'). The program does not move along chronologically. Rather, simultaneously developing subplots are presented, in soap opera fashion, and my accounting reflects this fragmentation.

Episode 1

Li arrives by train in a village said to be the capital of fictionalized Gulin County, part of a poor, dry farming area that bears a strong resemblance to Shanxi Province, home of the author. Li is a young Communist Party member from Beijing. He has been sent to Gulin County to become Party Secretary there. He is met by the Party Vice Secretary, Gu, a much older man, who will become Li's antagonist throughout the series. According to the bureaucratic structure, Li is Gu's boss. But Gu's older brother, Heng, is Party Secretary of the province in which Gulin County is located. To make things more interesting, Li's father, Haitao, has an even higher administrative post in Beijing. Beyond this, they all know each other from the days of the Communist Revolution.

Li and Gu must work together in Gulin and there is much work to be done as the county has a very poor reputation for productivity. Upon Li's arrival, Gu advises him about protocol in accomplishing their work: 'Don't talk too much . . . don't criticize past work . . . proceed slowly, listen, and follow me. You may have trouble if you

Photos 6.2 and 6.3: The series presents a classic confrontation between the 'new star', Li Xianlan (above), and his adversary, the old *ganbu*, Gu Rong.

go too fast'. Gu further advises that no changes should be made immediately, that 'research' should be conducted first. Li politely disagrees: 'No, we can do both at the same time'. Gu confides to a friend, 'Li cannot be controlled by anyone'. We begin to see big differences in their personalities and leadership styles. Li is the straight-talking intellectual who is concerned with fairness. Gu is the manipulative veteran bureaucrat – the classic stereotype of the incompetent *ganbu*.

In their first concrete struggle, Li orders analysis of a problem revealed by a woman who claims she has been discriminated against in her work by her *ganbu*. Li wants to know how many cases like this exist. To Gu's great embarrassment, his own son is implicated in the problem as a smuggler of antiques as is the son of one of Gu's fellow cadre, Feng. A continuing theme throughout the program is that Gu is somehow involved in many unsavory activities in the county. There is a constant blurring between bureaucratic privilege and illegal activity for Gu. He appears to be motivated by personal interest while Li is the people's advocate.

A town meeting is held where Li is introduced and is obliquely criticized by Gu for his aggressive style. Li addresses the crowd: 'The work here is not done efficiently. You don't serve the people. The Communist Party says "take care of the heart and soul of the people". We must support the people.'

Lin, Li's former girlfriend from their teenage days during the Cultural Revolution, arrives in Gulin. So does the attractive Shaoli, who is Gu's niece. Lin is portrayed as soft while Shaoli is tougher – aggressive and ambitious. Lin is a journalist. Shaoli, who is ten years younger, also wants to be a writer. She meets Li and immediately begins arguing with him, testing him. An intriguing tension between the two develops. There are some things to explain. Li is not married. At his age, apparently the early thirties, this is unusual in China. If someone is not married he must have some problem. A bad temper or incorrigible personality? Too personally ambitious? Why isn't Li married?

Episode 2

Li appoints a new director of policy research to replace an old *ganbu* who would not do the work the way Li wanted it done. Li then walks among the villagers to get the general feeling of the situation. He meets Shaoli on the street. During their conversation, Shaoli asks Li if he likes the clothes she is wearing and he tells her that they may be too modern, not appropriate for the farm country. A romance, however understated, seems to be blooming.

Li meets a poor woman who had come to tell him a story of the tragedy of her husband's death. She pleas for financial and medical help and says that she has walked 25 miles from her home to the county government headquarters more than fifty times in her previous efforts to get help from Gu, before Li arrived in Gulin, but received no attention. She claims that she had been unable to 'prove' to Gu her need for help. Li comforts her, assures her that she need not prove her need, saying that all those trips by foot are proof enough. This is a critical incident in the story because it reflects Li's personal caring and his ability to cut through the bureaucracy to act immediately. This leadership style contrasts with the old style personified by Gu, and suggests the potential of the reformation. Word circulates quickly among the people in Gulin that Li is a true friend of the common people. He is becoming a cultural hero. Shaoli watches Li from a distance, obviously becoming more and more interested in him.

Another mass meeting is held. By now the people are aware of Li's work and some of them have high expectations for the future. But Gu has been an official in the county for more than 30 years. They fear his power. Gu addresses them: 'Raise your hand if you are a Communist Party member!' Many hands are raised. Gu then indirectly criticizes Li (who is also present) claiming that experience, not youth, is what China needs. He reminds the group of the failure of the Great Leap Forward of 1958, attributing the problems of that era to the lack of wise leadership. He praises the comrades for their 'good recent work' and reminds them that he has 'never moved from this county'. He asks, 'Would someone else neglect our success here?' This episode ends with Li moving to the podium where he begins to address the group. Li gives a kind of pep talk, encouraging the people to try to be the top-producing county in China. He suggests that the great hopes for the future can only be accomplished through reform. The battle lines are clearly, but politely, drawn at this meeting as Gu and Li vie for the support of the party membership and for the confidence of the rest of the people of Gulin County.

Photos 6.4 and 6.5: Li walks among the people of Gulin County as Shaoli, below, keeps a close eye on him.

Episode 3

We resume with Li still addressing the Communist Party meeting. He remarks that the old leaders have made a fine contribution to the county, but now it is time for new challenges.

In the next scene, Gu is at home when the director and assistant director of the county police department arrive. The police have come to Gu's house to arrest his son (who is not at home) for smuggling. A long conversation ensues where Gu tries to convince the police to 'go easy' on his son. Thinking that the police may have been buoyed in their confidence to arrest his son by the presence of Li, Gu reminds them that Li is likely to leave: 'When he leaves, you will again be under my control', he tells them. The situation becomes further complicated when the police director's assistant asks Gu for help moving his wife from the countryside to the city to join him. And when it is revealed that the police director's son is ill, Gu offers to find help for him, but suggests that in return his own son should be taken care of as well: 'You should understand my feeling for my son!' Later, Gu literally falls ill at home under the pressure of the situation and is rushed by ambulance to a hospital. Li arrives at the hospital to pay his respects to the older, and apparently infirm, Gu.

Li walks among the people of the city, stopping to advise many of them how they can improve their personal finances through profit-driven, incentive-based work. He meets an old man, Se, whom he promises to help build a well to provide the much-needed water. The old man prefers to build a 'dragon temple' in order to pray for rain, but Li gently recommends that science is a better bet. Shaoli is watching Li during all these interactions, and she tells him, 'I want to write about you in my book'. He replies: 'No, you should write about Se instead'.

A loud dinner party is being held at the county electric company facility. The party is given in honor of the district leader of electric power who is visiting Gulin County. Li arrives and the festivities stop. He criticizes the electric company *ganbu* for inviting so many people to this party where the food and alcohol is paid for out of the department budget. He blames the *ganbu* for his failure to provide electricity to farmers who needed it for their harvests. By spending money on the party, Li said, 'You drink the people's blood'. A discussion takes place about how farmers have had to bribe the *ganbu* with gifts in order to get electricity. Li instructs that this practice must stop.

Photos 6.6 and 6.7: The people's advocate, Li listens to the problems of a woman who has been ignored by Gu. Below, Li counsels Se about building a well for water.

In the meantime, Gu is holding an unauthorized meeting in his hospital room with friends, many of whom are older *ganbu* who feel threatened by Li's presence in the county. They unite to oppose Li and agree with Gu's assessment that Li 'does not respect older officials'.

Episode 4

Several short scenes are shown. Gu telephones the district Party Secretary to complain about Li's 'troublemaking'. Li has a positive talk with the *ganbu* of the electric company, whom he had scolded previously, signalling that Li is winning respect from at least some of the managers. Li also solves a problem at a school where coal was needed to heat the children's food and drink.

The relationship between Li and his former girlfriend, Lin, is revealed at a public meeting. Li agrees to go public about their history and he goes to Lin's house but she isn't there. They meet by chance in the woods. With romantic music playing in the background, Li and Lin walk their bicycles along a path in the woods talking intimately about their past, about the situation in Gulin County, and about their life philosophies. Li is optimistic about changes in the party and in the country; Lin is cynical. They reach Lin's house and go inside. Li is smoking Winston (American-made) cigarettes and they share a western beverage, cocoa. Lin cries about her suffering during the Cultural Revolution. Li, expressing sadness that he had not taken more responsibility for Lin when they were young, listens to her sensitively as they discuss their roles in life – past, present, and future. It is clear that they do not have a romantic relationship any more, and Lin asks Li not to return to the house for fear of damaging both their reputations. They touch hands as he leaves.

Shaoli, meanwhile, has been following Li and Lin and appears to be very jealous when she sees them touch. In another brief scene, the police have arrived at Gu's house where, after all, they arrest his son.

Episode 5

Li and Shaoli walk together and the depth of their growing involvement becomes clear. They talk about the politics of the county and Li credits Shaoli for her maturity. 'To accomplish the reformation', he says, 'we must be strong'. Shaoli kisses Li on the cheek.

Photos 6.8 and 6.9: Li stops an extravagant party at the electric company because he thinks it's a waste of money. Below, the company *ganbu* tries to win Li's favor by toasting him, but Li won't have anything to do with it.

In brief scenes, Li visits the home of a retired *ganbu* to solicit support from him in his reform efforts. Gu contemplates writing a letter to Li's father to ask him to recall his son from the county. Li and Shaoli visit Gu to ask his advice on a small matter and Gu refuses to co-operate: 'I have no advice for you. Do what you want'.

Li travels to an outlying farm area by bus. He stops the bus to settle a fight between two female merchants. On the bus he discusses with others the problems that old Guomidang officials face in China today and he recommends improving their lot. A long discussion takes place at a water storage area in the countryside. Li wants to use the water that is contained by the dam to breed fish, a plan the party had already approved. The *ganbu* in charge of the dam is a former party official of the county who was dispatched to this undesirable job by Gu. The *ganbu* says that no progress has been made at the dam site in the plan for fish breeding because of bureaucratic hassles created by Gu.

Episode 6

Li continues to discuss the fish-breeding plan with Zhu, the official at the site. Li tells him, 'Before, it was the harder you worked, the more you got hurt. But with me here now this won't happen again.'

A struggle erupts between Li and the leader of a commune in the county, Pan, who was promoted to his position during the Cultural Revolution and is an old friend of Gu. Pan attempts to turn the people of his commune against Li by blaming him for the shortage of water suffered by the people of the commune. The people yell their disapproval at Li when he arrives. Li and Pan have a confrontation. Li tells Pan: 'It is your responsibility to solve the problem here. If you cannot do it, I will find another commune leader'. Li tells him that he is aware of the many awards that Pan received during the Cultural Revolution: 'But now is now. You must do your work. What research have you done?' The confrontation continues as Li and Pan visit a school house that has been destroyed by bad weather. Shoeless children and their teacher are forced to endure unbearable conditions at the school. Showing great concern for them, Li asks Pan: 'Why haven't you fixed this problem?' Pan responds that it is not his responsibility. Li tells him, '*You* are the director here. *You* are responsible!' Li turns to the teacher and the children and gives them a little speech, saying that the problem must be solved right away. The Li/Pan entourage continues to inspect the commune facilities. Li finds another room that could be used as a classroom, but Pan says it can't be done right away. Li asks Pan if he is really qualified to be a commune director. We also learn that Pan's nephew wants to marry the teacher and, if she doesn't agree, she will be reassigned to an even more undesirable place.

Episode 7

Another problem develops. Not only is the farming area in Gulin County lacking rain, Li discovers that the peasants have not been managing the land properly. The farmers explain to Li that they prefer to exploit the fields for immediate profits permitted under the new incentive policy. Conserving the land, rotating crops, and guarding against erosion are long-term approaches to farming. But because the peasants fear that the 'incentive' policy will be revoked or changed in the near future, they have made the short-term decision to get as much immediate gain as possible. This scene reveals another serious problem that plagues the country – the lack of faith that people have in the consistency and stability of government policy. To solve this problem with respect to local farming, Li appoints Hu, a *ganbu* with whom he had disagreed earlier and who had called Li's attention to the land management problem, to a high-level research position. This appointment reflects on Li's fairness (appointing a former opponent) and his practicality (appointing a talented and hard-working person to a key post – a key contrast to the stereotype of positions held by unqualified *ganbu*).

We briefly meet Uncle Meng, a shabby old man who lives in the forest and advocates protection of the woodlands (he will return later). Li goes back to the village where the elementary school is located to see if Pan had made the improvements he demanded. As Li approaches, the old school collapses, injuring many children. The teacher lies nearly dead. Emergency vehicles are not available for the rescue attempt as they are all being used by the director of the hospital for unauthorized personal reasons.

Throughout these scenes we see that several local committee members of the Communist Party are beginning to support Li. They vote to fire Pan from his position as secretary of the commune – a major show of support for Li. Li then makes a speech at a party meeting where he appoints Hu, the former adversary who had already been promoted, to the position. Further demonstrating

Photos 6.10 and 6.11: Li and Gu talk about Li's future in Gulin County, while, below, Li and Shaoli share a lighter moment together.

kindness and fairness, Li consoles Pan in the speech, reminding the group that 'every *ganbu* should learn a lesson from what has happened here'. In the final scene, Li is back on the bus headed to the countryside when a storm breaks out and a tree falls across the road.

Episode 8

We resume the story back on the road where it is apparent that there has been much illegal cutting of trees. This is a big problem in China as about one-fourth of the nation's forests have been destroyed since the Liberation. Young men are using a government truck to haul the stolen wood. Li busts them at this, but he patiently explains to them what they are doing is wrong. The way Li handles the situation stands in stark contrast to the heavy-handed tactics typically used by the old *ganbu*.

Uncle Meng, the old man of the forest, is in his little house. He is portrayed as a kind old man with a habit of conserving everything – he will take nothing for himself and his love of the woodlands is evidence of his selflessness. He is later shown in the forest admiring the birds and animals, when he encounters a group of boys. He asks them not to hunt or smoke so as to protect the trees.

A struggle takes place when many young men prepare to return to the forest in order to illegally cut trees again. Uncle Meng tries to stop them, but falls and hurts himself on some rocks. In another location, Li discusses with experts the wisdom of tree cutting. Another former adversary of Li contributes to the discussion, a subtle indication of his growing support for Li. The *ganbu* who allowed the tree cutting is fired.

Episode 9

In the firing of the incompetent *ganbu*, Li lectures the gathering about protecting the forest. At the time he praises the contribution made by the old *ganbu*, but he says that 'you have lost control here' and he tells him 'now you can do other important work'.

Shaoli brings her uncle Gu a letter that is written by Li's father, the head of a central ministry in Beijing. We find out that Gu had written a polite letter to the senior Li previously, complaining about his son. Shaoli is upset with her uncle's actions. Hu, the *ganbu* who twice had been promoted by Li, shows up and he and Gu begin to discuss the younger Li's performance in the county. Hu: 'We should take care of the people.' Gu: 'We are politicians. We should take care of political problems.' Shaoli and Gu fight after she reads the letter aloud. In the letter, the elder Li allows that his son may not be competent for the position he has assumed. Shaoli angrily departs to find Li. She runs into Lin along the way and they have unpleasant words.

Pan, the fired commune secretary, cries at home about the loss of his job. Some children from the village laugh at him and a man tries to collect money from him for some painting that had been done. This scene makes the point that when Pan held his position as secretary, he would not have had to pay for the work, but instead would have granted the painter a favor – an abuse of power and reliance on relationships that is typical of the old *guanxi*-based system.

We resume action in the forest. Uncle Meng is gravely injured by his fall but many young men are still intent on cutting trees. Meng's son begs the men not to do it. Li arrives and he and Gao, a *ganbu* in charge of the forest, have a confrontation. Gao offers to resign and there is a taking of sides over him. A generational difference emerges as he is supported, at least tolerated, by the older men but is opposed by the younger ones. Li tells him, 'You have worked hard, but the masses oppose you now. You should absorb a lesson from this.' Li then addresses the young men about the history of the county, and they admit that they are wrong.

Li now realizes that he knows who old Uncle Meng is. Forty years ago the old man had saved Li's father's life. After that, Meng had singlehandedly planted all the trees nearby, turning a bare mountain into a forest. In the final scene, Meng is dying from his fall. Meng refuses to admit that he had helped Li's father (an indication of his selflessness), but requests that a box full of money that he has saved throughout his life be used for protecting the forest, *not* for his son or grandson. Li promises that the money will be spent accordingly.

Episode 10

Uncle Meng dies and many people come by the house to pay their respects. A variety of short scenes follow. Shaoli gives Li a letter from his father. Gu and his wife go to the jail to visit their son. The jailed son asks his father to get him out, and old Gu answers: 'I can't do more under the law. Your daddy's heart is very sad.'

Pan later comes to Gu's house, crying pathetically (an unacceptable show of emotion in this situation for a Chinese man) and looking for sympathy.

Shaoli is plotting for a way to convince her father to support Li. Gu notices that Shaoli has written Li's name on some papers in her room (she lives in her uncle Gu's house). Gu asks Shaoli of her feelings about Li:

Gu: 'There have been lots of rumors.'
Shaoli: 'I don't care.'
Gu: 'Do you have a special feeling for Li?'
Shaoli: 'I want to live with him.'
Gu: 'And what of Li's feelings about you?'
Shaoli: 'He is kind to me.'
Gu: 'But there are political considerations . . .'
Shaoli: 'I don't want anyone else to take care of me.'
Gu: 'But what about Li's relationship with Lin?'
Shaoli: 'I don't care. What I want to do is up to me.'

This exchange is a clear illustration of an extremely untraditional position taken by a woman in the People's Republic and contrasts vividly with the style of the older and far more conservative Lin.

The next day Shaoli goes out to find Li, but runs into a friend who warns her that Li may be leaving the county soon. Shaoli yells, 'No!' She runs to the outskirts of town where she finds Li walking with Lin. She jealously watches them. They notice Shaoli and Lin touches Li as she departs from him, asking him to visit her. Li asks Shaoli why she came there. Shaoli is nearly hysterical, threatening to kill herself. Li asks her to sit and talk. He tells her that he wants to contribute something positive to the history of China. She says that she will ask her father, Secretary of the Province (the next administrative level) to help him, saying she has designed a clever strategy for doing so. Li tells her he doesn't want this kind of help. Shaoli threatens Li, telling him that she can hurt him by revealing his relationship to Lin who now is revealed to have been married to Shaoli's brother and was sexually abused as a teenager! Li angrily stands up and asks her why must she be so hard? Why can't she take pity on a divorcee? He asks Shaoli why she cannot understand another person's position. He tells her that she is very lovely, but that she also makes people suffer – 'this is such a contradiction'. Shaoli runs away. In the final scene, a train arrives in Gulin County carrying Zheng, a high-level party official and the former Secretary of Gulin County, a man who once held the position that is now occupied by Li.

Episode 11

Zheng has arrived to check Li's work and he immediately gets bad impressions. Shaoli runs into Zheng and Li and acts as if she doesn't really know Li. They meet workers from the electric company who had their privileges curtailed by Li earlier for their excessive partying. Gu invites Zheng home for dinner where they meet with other 'resistors' to Li to discuss a strategy for possibly removing Li. Zheng claims that he (Zheng) is democratic. He says, for instance, that his wife and children decide about what food is eaten in his home. Despite his politeness and apparent correctness, however, Zheng opposes the reformation and asks Li to give it up.

An executive party committee meeting is held to discuss Li's future. Li, who is present, is criticized on two counts. First, one of his adversaries claims that Li has failed to acknowledge contributions made by former officials (including Zheng, but also Gu) to the progress of the county. Second, Li is called a 'dictator', that he makes all the decisions by himself and as a result the people feel oppressed. Li denies the charges.

Hu speaks on Li's behalf, giving an account of his own transformation and outlining the problems with Gu's son. He asks Zheng to be objective. Another man, an intellectual, supports Li, saying 'some officials do nothing', a remark that Zheng takes personally. Several other key committee members speak in support of Li, including the *ganbu* from the electric company who earlier had been busted by Li. This is a crucial moment in the drama as it is nearly impossible to imagine in real life that a *ganbu* who had been embarrassed and punished as this man had would support the person responsible. The portrayal of many *ganbu* in *New Star* is ultimately favorable, showing their potential for acceptance of the new leadership style embodied in the character of Li Xianlan.

Li explains the reasoning behind his decisions during the two months of his governance in the county. When some questions are directed to him about his involvement with Lin and Shaoli, however, he abruptly stands and leaves the room. In private later, friends encourage Li to speak out and extinguish the rumors about his relationships with the women. Li loses control emotionally in front of his friends, but calms down and quietly remarks that 'we must continue our work here, otherwise we fail'. At the end of the episode one of Li's confidants finds out from the director of the police station that Zheng has ordered Li transferred out of the county.

Episode 12

Several short scenes introduce the last episode. Li's friends try to convince Zheng to support him. Li arrives at the room where Zheng is staying but cannot talk to him because Zheng is watching a volleyball match on television and ignores him. Feng is at home celebrating the news of Li's departure as he thinks this will clear the way to have his son (who had been incarcerated with Gu's son for smuggling) released from jail. Shaoli and Li meet briefly. She is leaving by bus and Li asks her to say 'hello' to her father. Zheng and Li finally meet to discuss the situation. Zheng tells him he is going to 'change your position' and also advises him to be more careful with his girlfriends.

Li and one of his closest friends, Kang, have coffee together, then take a walk. Kang consoles him, telling him he is 'too good' and threatens people like Zheng. Li claims that he himself is not competent for political work, but Kang insists that his talent is both theoretical and practical and urges him to stay and contribute. They discuss Li's romantic situation, and Li admits that perhaps he should be married. Kang says someday he will write a novel about Li. He says the title will be, *Ambitious and Loving*.

Li goes to visit Lin who receives him warmly. Their relationship has changed now with Li's firing. Lin is a 'damaged woman' because of her past (especially the divorce) and Li is damaged now too. They are closer as a result. Li tells her he wants to find a more quiet environment and continue to do some research on Chinese social and political problems. They walk together to visit an old woman who had taken care of Li when he was a young boy. They greet the woman who then prepares Li's favorite food which she remembers from years ago. Li gives her a present of clothes and distributes little gifts to the other neighbors. Everyone knows that Li is leaving and they are sad.

Again, Li and Lin walk together. They discuss their philosophies and recall the time they had spent together as teenagers. They talk about the political realities of making an impact at the highest level in China. Family politics are discussed too and Lin clearly explains her past marriage, a description that upsets Li. They meet a group of *ganbu* who are supportive of Li. The *ganbu* ask him not to leave the county, but he asks them to support his *work*, not him. Much support is shown for Li by his former opponents and by those who previously had not taken a position.

A bicyclist approaches with a letter from the Secretary of the Province, the brother of Gu and the father of Shaoli. The letter praises Li, saying, 'You have some good ideas, good proposals [for reform]. I gave a copy of your proposals to all province party committee members to read.' So, ironically, Li is being dismissed from his position, but receives praise at the same time.[2] *New Star* ends ambiguously. Li is supported as a 'new generation leader' and the reformation seems to have been implicitly endorsed. Still, Li's personal future is in doubt and the potential for Gulin County's reformation is also unclear.

AUDIENCE RESPONSE TO *NEW STAR* – THE REFORMATION IN FASHION

'This is a program that discloses a problem. It's not just a positive representation or a funny escape.' (28-year-old female cellist in orchestra, Guangzhou)

'We were happy to see this program. Now we don't have to hold this feeling inside any more.' (61-year-old female retired textile worker, Xian)

'*New Star* helped encourage young people to fight the problem. The program reflects the will of the people.' (62-year-old male teacher in a telecommunications institute, Shanghai)

'It was a show about ordinary people. If someone can support us, we like to watch it.' (40-year-old male machinist, Beijing)

'This program shows the truth – the mistreatment of farmers and workers.' (28-year-old female unemployed worker, Beijing)

'We didn't watch it. We didn't like it. I don't even like the *New Star* theme song.' (33-year-old male driver for the post office, Beijing)

Almost everyone in China had an opinion about *New Star*. The great majority of the comments were favorable, and many reasons were expressed for liking the series. But there were lots of criticisms too, even among the show's fans. One point is clear: the program caught the attention of the world's largest television audience because of its subject matter. The social researcher who coined the term '*New Star* fever', described the program as 'acupuncture that touched the contemporary social dilemma in China' (Zhou 1986). The audience responded at several levels. They were fully aware of the program's political sensitivities and its relevance to their everyday lives. They were also attracted to the program simply because there are so few domestic drama series on the television system at all. And, as we shall see, many reacted strongly to the lead character, Li Xianlan.

ZHOU'S STUDY

I was told by faculty members at the People's University in Beijing about a graduate student in the Department of Sociology at Beijing University who was about to publish a major piece of survey research on the audience's response to *New Star*. This man is Zhou Yong-ping. We met with Zhou to discuss his study and to translate into English an article he was writing about his research that was subsequently published in a Chinese journal (Zhou 1986). Zhou's work is important for two reasons. Not only does it disclose systematic information about this television series, but the very fact that the study was conducted and published indicates China's serious scholarly interest in mass communication.

Zhou sensed from the beginning that *New Star* was important. Word of mouth about the series was so strong that he developed a survey questionnaire in order to measure public opinion about the show. He met with officials at TYTV, the author of the story (Kuo Yun Lu), and workers at various levels (farmers, factory and service workers, technical specialists, professionals, and students) in order to decide what items should be included in the questionnaire. He mailed copies of the questionnaire to a random sample of 1,300 people in Beijing and Shanghai, including the outlying regions where farmers live. Some 849 of the questionnaires were returned (75.3 percent) and, according to Zhou, unrecovered questionnaires were missing because of administrative problems in the research rather than lack of enthusiasm for the program.

THE OVERALL RESPONSE

New Star's enormous popularity was clearly evident both in my research and in Zhou's. Nearly every family we talked to knew about the program and most had watched several episodes. The national television network – which depends on letters sent in from the audience as its primary source of information about viewer preferences – had never received so many letters about any program. Some 92 percent of the opinions expressed were favorable. Zhou reports that 90.9 percent of the people who responded to his survey watched at least one of the episodes and that about half his respondents watched them all. Of Zhou's respondents who watched, 91 percent said they liked the show.[3] Chinese print media published countless positive reviews. People throughout China talked about the program at home and at work.

Zhou found that the program was popular among all viewers including, believe it or not, most *ganbu*, though they and high school students (for a very different reason – lack of interest) were least favorable toward the program. Besides the relevance of the program to life in China, the two major factors that encouraged viewing were the series format (audiences became hooked on the show after viewing one episode) and interpersonal influence attributable to the favorable talk that the program stimulated.

HOW *NEW STAR* PLAYED REGIONALLY

While the program was widely appreciated throughout China, *New Star* was not received with equal enthusiasm everywhere. The most interest and favorable response came from the north-central part of the country, as measured by letters sent to CCTV, the high ratings it received in Zhou's research (which was conducted there), and the interest and knowledge expressed by our narrators from this area.

Southern Chinese viewers generally were less influenced by *New Star*. The moderate reaction in Guangzhou, for instance, is understandable given the city's reputation as an island unto itself in China, where official matters in far-off Beijing and the policy dictates of the Communist Party are far less central to everyday life than they are elsewhere. The emergence of the comparatively large 'private unit' economic sector in Guangzhou, the relatively developed city atmosphere (in contrast to the farms and villages of north-central China that are portrayed on the program), the proximity of the city to China's special economic zones, and the influence of nearby Hong Kong (including its transmission of western-style TV dramas that can be received in Guangzhou) all made *New Star* less relevant to many residents of the southern city.

Still, *New Star* appeared twice on television in Guangzhou and

Guangdong Province and, according to broadcast authorities, the program was popular overall and had a significant impact. The Guangdong station originally carried the Mandarin-language version from the national network. Many viewers wanted to see it again in Cantonese. The Guandong Province television station repeated the show, translating it into the regional language and adding subtitles.

HOW REALISTIC IS *NEW STAR*?

'Realism' is a key evaluative criterion raised by viewers. Various realisms emerged. First, the audience frequently told us that the very presence of the reformation issue on television is realistic because it brings fundamental social problems and possible solutions fully to the attention of the public via television, the nation's most effective communication medium. In Zhou's survey, 78 percent of the respondents agreed that 'a realistic picture of the main conflict in contemporary Chinese society was presented (in *New Star*)'. Even more (79 percent) agreed with the statement: '*New Star* deeply revealed the necessity of the reformation; it reflects the people's strong desire for the reformation'. Zhou's study also shows that viewers (77 percent) thought that the program realistically portrays the *resistance* that the reformation faces. And, respondents did not agree that *New Star* 'describes (Chinese) society too darkly' (3 percent) or that the 'political conflict in the Communist Party' was 'too exaggerated' in the program (3 percent).

After this general endorsement of *New Star*'s realism, however, many audience members said that the way in which the reformation was portrayed in *New Star* is far less true to life:

'Our family watched this program from our hearts. But this kind of reformation is not possible in our department.' (26-year-old female worker in publishing company, Beijing)

'The direction of the reformation is correct (but) from an economic standpoint we can't promote the living standard very fast. The drama was exaggerated.' (44-year-old male *ganbu* for harbor workers, Guangzhou)

'If you try to act this way (Li's style), you won't survive in my department. The social pressure is too strong. A friend of mine made a proposal titled, "Making the Unreasonable Policy More Reasonable". He was criticized by his *ganbu*, pushed out of the picture, ignored, and considered to be a troublemaker who was

breaking up harmony and morale at work. But in reality my
friend made a very good suggestion about management and economic development.' (22-year-old male hotel service worker,
Beijing)

'I didn't like *New Star*. The leader corrected the problems in one
or two days. That's impossible and unrealistic.' (15-year-old male
high school student, Beijing)

So, while *New Star* was thought to be realistic in its portrayal of
problems that are close to home, *the way problems were solved* in
the drama was far less convincing. It is important to explore reasons
behind viewers' complaints that *New Star* unrealistically portrays
the way the reformation is being carried out. These perceptions
signal much more than feelings about a television program.

Certainly one reason for the audience's discomfort with this
aspect of the story results from the adaptation of the novel into a
television program. Key scenes are included in a very concentrated
way. The program often seems to be a series of incredible disasters
or sticky situations that are almost always effectively solved quickly
by Li. His brusque efficiency, exacerbated by the compression of
time and action characteristic of television drama, made this aspect
of the story seem unbelievable to some viewers. While some people
fantasized about how China could benefit from such an uncharacter-
istic speeding up of change, others were less certain of the possibility. Consider this difference of opinion:

'The problems (that are raised) in the show are true and part of
our daily life. This program should be repeated. We need a wide
ax to do the reformation work. If the country can do it this way,
then we can develop fast. We only have a strong policy on paper.
It seems like we can never really do it, finish it. Are we lazy?
Always delayed? Slow? This may be our Chinese habit, our
personality.' (56-year-old female retired seamstress, Beijing)

'The program is not true. Not all second generation leaders are
like Li. His behavior is too strong and he is not part of the
people. The reformation must take place from the top down.
Li's behavior was too radical. My friends and myself make our
contribution by doing our jobs well. What he did was not realistic.
He was not like most people in his position.' (37-year-old female
medical doctor, Beijing, and daughter of a high-ranking Communist Party official)

GUANXI IN SERVICE OF THE REFORMATION

Ironically, several viewers believed that one of the most serious social problems in China and one of the central themes criticized in *New Star* – the dependence on personal relationships – actually is necessary to advance the goals of the reformation:

> '. . . it was not realistic that one man can complete the reformation. To do this you need the support of the people, and good support in your relationships too. It's not so easy . . . you can't just point your finger at things and demand change. In this way the drama made it look too simple.' (66-year-old male retired carpenter, Beijing)

One couple, both party members, also evaluated the realism of the program – and the potential of the reformation – by emphasizing the importance of personal relationships in the work setting. They launched into a thoughtful critique of the program and engaged in a discussion of how they think the reformation can be accomplished according to party policy:

> *Wife*: 'The novel may be more deep. The television drama reflects only the basic idea. A young leader must belong to a unit. One person cannot fire or appoint another person by himself. It is not one person's right. So, the show was not realistic, not true.'
>
> *Husband*: 'For example, even the lead character (Li) depended on a relationship to become a leader. And he depended on a relationship to get his support. Then he turned his back on this relationship-based system.'
>
> *Wife*: 'Of course young leaders will make their changes, but we should respect the history and contributions of the older generation. So, the strategy Li used is not acceptable. He is 20-something years old and already he's dogmatic. What will he be like when he's 50?'
>
> *Husband*: 'The reformation will take place through relationships. Without the support of friends, there is no hope for reformation. Existing relationships must be used to evolve to a new structure. Of course there is some corruption in the Communist Party, but most of the old members are very good. They need to be gently educated or phased out. New leaders can still learn from the old ones.' (Husband: 51-year-old personnel supervisor in teacher education, a *ganbu*, Beijing; Wife: 48-year-old elementary school teacher, Beijing)

LI XIANLAN – PERSONIFICATION OF THE REFORMATION

Not all of the families that we interviewed in China remembered *New Star* by its title, but as soon as we mentioned Li's name there would usually be instant recognition. His name became synonymous with the program and, in the mind of many viewers, with the reformation. Of course Li *is* the 'new star'. And while most people said they admired him, his heroism was flawed. As we have seen, many viewers complained that he got his executive position as in the province only because of the privilege provided by the position of his father – a kind of relationship abuse. Because of this, Li's accomplishments in the program were considered by some viewers to be tainted or, to continue the theme I am already developing, unrealistic. Comments such as these were common:

'. . . if we put this story into our real life it is not possible. He had power because of his father.' (28-year-old male food store worker, Beijing)

'An ordinary-status person cannot accomplish what Li did. His father was a high leader. Only in this kind of situation can someone do what he did. If somebody else tried this, the person would be stopped. Most people support Li, the character, but the reality is far more complicated.' (36-year-old female accountant, Beijing)

'There should be examinations for young leaders. Who can solve China's problems? Nobody should depend on their father or the status of the Communist Party to occupy a job they would not otherwise have' (42-year-old battery salesman, Beijing)

There were other criticisms of Li too. One Beijing woman, a 55-year-old retired cook, called him 'wild, stubborn, and unreasonable. He tries to give a little lesson to anyone he can find. Anyway, I never met anybody like him in my whole life.' True enough, Li is different – an exceptional leader who stands out because he so aggressively pursues a policy and course of action he believes is right. Traditionally in Chinese society, individuals who promote themselves or their points of view too strongly are disliked or thought to be foolish. But most viewers of *New Star* praised Li for his aggressive and rather self-righteous personality. They often spoke of him as a friend. They said they could participate vicariously in the reformation through him.

Li's role as a leader in the reformation together with television's penchant for making stars through repeated exposure and the feeling of intimacy produced by the melodrama's close-up style had created a media hero. The image of Li surpassed any of the constructed 'model citizen' personae of highly planned campaigns originating in the Department of Propaganda:

'I respect Li. He is so successful. When he says something he never changes his direction. He is a real man . . . a strong personality. Li has so many qualities in one person. He is a symbol of many virtues.' (22-year-old military vehicle mechanic, Xian)

This remark reflects the primary perceptions that audience members held toward Li: strength and fairness. Our narrators described Li's strength this way: 'decisive', 'had courage . . . he dared to say and dared to do', 'powerful just like he should be', 'clear and strong', 'didn't hesitate', 'grasps situations tightly', 'strong mind', 'says what is right and doesn't care about pressure', and 'not afraid'. Furthermore, some 92 percent of Zhou's respondents agreed with the statement: 'Li is a confident, powerful, and talented person; when he handles problems he is strong and insistent'.

Just as important, he was considered to be fair: '(he) listens to public opinion . . . doesn't just make decisions by himself', 'keeps his promise . . . he can really bring the "higher spirit" to the low workers', 'fair . . . works on behalf of the ordinary people', 'honest', and 'made mistakes, but corrected his mistakes'. In Zhou's report, 74 percent of the sample agreed that 'Li never takes advantage of the system; he is a good official to protect the people'. Only 2 percent agreed with the assertion that 'Li is politically devious; he wants private profit'. Several of our narrators complimented Li highly by referring to him as a *Bao chieng tien* personality. Bao was a famous judge who lived during the Song Dynasty and was known for his absolute fairness. *Chieng tien* means 'clear sky' or 'blue sky'. Li Xianlan protected the rights of uneducated farmers and workers, just as Judge Bao had done centuries before. Li had earned the honorific title from history, *Bao chieng tien*.

Li gave symbolic hope to many viewers that the Chinese reformation might someday begin to resemble in reality what took place in *New Star*. Nearly everyone we talked to said they believed that the 'tendency' of the reformation as it was displayed in *New Star* is correct. After that, however, opinion was divided between those who wishfully believed that it might be possible to accomplish the work in a manner similar to what was shown, those who believed that it was unrealistic to expect anything of the sort, and others who thought that the reformation could happen, but that Li's leadership style was inappropriate. This matter of style was discussed by several of our narrators:

'Li was like an idol . . . his image was that of a moving idol, not a person. I like his power and the way he worked against an unfair system . . . In all of China we have had only one real leader like Li (Ma Sen-li, a factory reform leader of the 1970s). Before he became famous he had a miserable life. Do you realize how much difficulty and frustration he experienced?' (33-year-old female electronics assembly worker, Beijing)

'I want the country to be strong. Everybody should support the reformation, but whether Li's style is correct is another question. In some ways we disagree with the way he did the work. He may have acted too fast.' (37-year-old male teacher in an industrial economics college and a party member, Xian)

'. . . the actor's style was not typical of a Communist Party member. When he first got the job he fired lots of people. The Communist Party does not act this way. We cannot do our work without thorough thinking . . . (Li) had a new solution for the situation, that's good, but the personality of his character is not good . . . The reformation needs a method to be effective . . . the party method must be structured, stable, and flexible.' (51-year-old male personnel supervisor, a *ganbu* and party member, Beijing)

'In reality we rarely even hope to have a hero like Li because this kind of person will have a lot of power directed against him.' (49-year-old male English teacher at a statistics college, Xian)

'(Li) is persistent, tenacious, and never discouraged, although he was short-tempered at times. But he is young. His technique is not sophisticated. So people criticize this part of his character, but nobody can deny that he is a model for the reformation. In the mind of the audience, he has an excellent reputation. People hope that all reformers can be like him – brave, intense, and able to push away all the stones that stand in the way of the reformation.' (39-year-old female college history professor, Guangzhou, and Communist Party member)

GU – PERSONIFICATION OF RESISTANCE TO THE REFORMATION

The audience also reacted strongly to Li's antagonist, Gu Rong. His role in the television series as the conservative, old *ganbu* represents a role in Chinese society that is far more recognizable to viewers than the image of Li had been. Whereas Li represents the ideal *ganbu*, Gu is the reality. In Zhou's research, the audience rated Gu's performance as more realistic than Li's, though it is difficult to know if the respondents were reacting to the ability of the actor or to the role he played in the program. The audience responded to Gu as a kind of 'composite' *ganbu*, a fictionalized character who possesses all the bad qualities of the middle-level bureaucrats, a man who combines the worst of Chinese tradition with the most corrupt and inefficient elements of the contemporary communist system. Respondents to Zhou's questionnaire said that while Gu's negative image should not be confused with all *ganbu* or with the Communist Party, they agreed strongly (83 percent) that 'In the real world we seldom see a person like Li, but we see many people like Gu and Pan' (the commune director who was dismissed by Li in the program).

CONCLUSIONS

New Star was more than a television series. As a political soap opera/docudrama, the program entertained millions of viewers while it simultaneously painted an artistically awkward but convincing critique of bureaucratic abuse that is very familiar and hated by many Chinese citizens. People rallied behind the program. Some saw it as a symbol of China's *spiritual* modernization, the ideological element of the current reform movement. The program inspired thoughts of the possibility of political change and economic prosperity – developments that many Chinese believe can only occur when the social problems dramatized so effectively in *New Star* are substantially reduced. In a way, *New Star* was a kind of attack that China brought upon itself. Interpretations that viewers made of the program reflected not only their feelings about the show, but about the future of the country.

BATTLEGROUND OF THE GENERATIONS?

As we have seen, the proper course for charting China's future is a highly subjective and controversial matter. Differences of opinion that were expressed about *New Star*, and about Li's leadership style, were often divided by age and generation within families. Generally, many members of the 'younger generation' (under 40) insist on reformation and believe that charismatic leaders like Li must lead the way. On the other hand, members of the older generation often prefer to keep the system in place, tolerating a slower pace for change. Our narrators provide additional perspectives:

'Well, there *is* a generation gap in China. Older people literally have different ideas from younger ones. The new generation wants reform and the old generation sometimes doesn't even recognize the problem.' (40-year-old male cybernetics engineer, Beijing)

'The old generation thinks that young men like Li are trying to steal power from the old. The young generation thinks that Li's attitude and actions were appropriate for the job.' (37-year-old male *ganbu* in a plastics factory, Guangzhou)

'Our father does not agree with us (the narrator and his 22-year-old brother) so he kept quiet while we all watched the show.' (26-year-old male roofer, Shanghai)

'When the program dealt with the relationship between the young and the old generation, it was not mature.' (36-year-old male news film editor, Beijing)

In some cases, however, members of the *older* generation are the ones that support the reform while their children are either not interested, think it doesn't apply to them, distrust the motives behind the movement, or are profoundly cynical about China's ability to transform such an entrenched system. Zhou's study casts light on this situation too. He found that people of all ages and work categories were favorable to reform, positive about *New Star*, and supportive of Li. He concludes that the generations overlap more than they differ. Given the strong commentaries made by family members we talked to, I am less certain about the extent of the overlap. I do agree that the effect was not completely demarcated according to age or generation and that some of the positions held by viewers, such as those mentioned above, encourage deeper analysis.

NEW STAR AND THE IDEOLOGICAL ROLE OF CHINESE MASS MEDIA

Literature in China, including the stories that the contemporary mass media tell, is supposed to serve a political purpose. Media hardware and software are agents for the intentional creation of certain public discourses. These discourses include various public introspections and self-criticisms. But other tactics are far more common. Mass media frequently promote blatant government positions on issues of all types.

Management of public media and public information, however, does not guarantee compliance. Several obstacles separate behavioral prescriptions particularly from public opinion and activity:

'Television should reflect the truth about our daily life. Let the people evaluate our situation.' (28-year-old male automobile factory worker, Shanghai)

The first objection is that Chinese television is perceived by many viewers as unwilling to present and discuss certain problems – including especially many of the issues raised in *New Star*. One perceived operating principle of Chinese media, therefore, is that of pro-active censorship – the creation of a controlled agenda that does not sufficiently address widely recognized trouble spots in Chinese society or that coverage of these themes is insufficiently specific and critical. The people say they want the media to be honest – to face society's problems in a straightforward way. Television is frequently criticized for failing to do this.

'The government has good ideals, good values, and good representations on the media but these cannot be used so easily in our work units. The *ganbu* will demand that the workers follow him, not the ideals.' (52-year-old male worker in a clock/watch factory, Shanghai)

'When the reformation starts to take place it is only temporary. Very soon everything goes back to the old situation. No matter how many TV dramas you produce, so what? It's never true in the society itself.' (26-year-old male worker in a mint, Shanghai)

A second major problem is the gap between the official rhetoric

of the government, including its media pronouncements, and conditions of life routinely experienced by citizens, especially at work.
Party policy often is not reflected accurately or sufficiently in the
management of day-to-day practices that constitute the core of
everyday life. As we have seen, this problem results partly from
the inability or unwillingness of middle-level *ganbu* to carry out the
official vision. But more generally, China suffers from vestiges of
certain well-established and debilitating traditions attributable to the
feudalist era and from slippages within today's socialist bureaucracy.
According to many people, these interacting factors prevent China
from reaching its potential, regardless of the high leaders' good
intentions and the utilitarian value of repeated recommendations
made on the mass media. One problem, then, is not whether the
people support the party, its leaders, and their plans, but the potential for realizing them. The difficulties are even more sharp and
prohibitive when major social changes, like those promised in the
rhetoric of the reformation, are at question.

'Media reports about the reformation are not really true. The
party just follows a form. Every department claims that it is
evolving, but it's just not true – it's just a hollow image.' (44-
year-old male worker in electrical power plant, Beijing)

'The reformation is new . . . we don't fully understand this stage
in our history. For China, we construct and experience the reformation all at the same time. We walk, we touch, we discover
problems . . .' (Wang Chuan-yu, Chief Editor, CCTV, Beijing)

A third objection that people have is that not only is China
developing too slowly, people are subjected to endless official
hyperbole that is designed to create an artificial image – an unrealistic, overly positive picture of current conditions. Some media
proclamations are evaluated suspiciously, even cynically, by many
citizens. For many people, the certainty of media representations
is not well matched with the tentativeness of government policy
and actual conditions of life.

The problem is *instability*. Equivocations concerning the direction
of the nation, the philosophy behind the creation and carrying out
of party policy, and uncertainties and broken promises surrounding
the rights of individuals in China are well understood and disliked
by many people. The reformation in general, and the 'modernization of thinking' in particular, have strong implications for democratic reform, and this is a very sensitive issue for Chinese. They

remember well that Mao's 'Hundred Flowers Movement' in 1957, which was designed to promote robust criticism of the government and its leaders in order to produce democratic dialogue, was followed later the same year by the oppressive Anti-Rightist Campaign where many people were persecuted for expressing political sentiments. More recent is the case of the famed 'Democracy Wall' in Beijing, a place where citizens were at one time permitted to express political opinion. It was closed unceremoniously in 1978. The student uprisings in late 1986 and early 1987 in Shanghai and Beijing were snuffed out by the government at the height of excitement about the 'open door' policy. Government battles with students crescendoed again in the spring of 1989. Unclear and constantly changing policy has not inspired confidence among many people in China. And, of course, memories of the most extreme period in the nation's recent history, the Cultural Revolution, remind everyone of the harshness with which policy – no matter how morally reprehensible and ineffective – may be enforced.

While high-level party officials may believe that they have steered a stable course for national development, the general perception among citizens is far less generous in its estimation of consistency. Many Chinese people believe that the bloated bureaucracy and history of political equivocations are somehow inherent in the culture, plagues whose roots can be traced to pre-socialist China, even to the early feudalist periods. The vast and complex nature of the Chinese reformation, whose internal conflicts were provocatively represented in *New Star*, takes place in the atmosphere I have described here. Interpretations of the program, and of the reformation itself, are influenced by these factors. Chinese mass media more than ever are implicated in the nation's complicated political scenario.

LI XIANLAN AND THE 'GREAT LEADER THEORY'

From Confucius to the feudal emperors, to Chiang Kai-Shek, Mao Zedong, Deng Xiaoping, and even Fang Lizhi, China calls out for heroes. Li Xianlan was China's first television hero. We have seen that many viewers admired him deeply, considered him a friend, and engaged him to do vicariously what they cannot do in their own work situations.

One critical argument that can be made *against New Star* as a symbol of the reformation, however, relates to Li's popularity. Many audience members may have seen the key to reform in the *person* of Li, rather than in any tuning or restructuring of the socialist system, democratic participation, or the redistribution of social power. The program may have reflected too much on the individual leader and his personal triumphs. The villagers and farmers of Gulin County thought Li was a savior – an authentic, modern-day judge *Bao Chieng Tien*. The audience's preoccupation with Li's leadership style, therefore, may have overshadowed analysis of the deeper difficulties, problems less amenable to the dramatic conventions and visual priorities of television. The system itself stayed in place during *New Star*. The rules were the same before and after Li's tenure in Gulin County.

FINAL THOUGHTS

New Star left everyone with lots of questions. First of all we don't know what happened to Li or to Gulin County. While Li was heroic, in the end he was not clearly successful. His removal from the county presumably left the fate of the people there in Gu's hands once again. Many viewers liked the show but didn't like the ending or preferred not to accept the hopelessness of the final scenes.

Still, the very appearance of *New Star* on the national television network is one of the most important and interesting developments to take place in China since the end of the Cultural Revolution. No other domestic program has ever stirred viewer interest like this one did. People took *New Star* personally. One woman remarked incredulously, 'finally somebody did something for us!' Family members talked about the program at home and at work, discussing not only the show's artistic merits and dramatic intrigues, but its relevance to their daily lives and the future of the whole country. Chinese men – like males all over the world – rarely discuss television dramas with each other, but they frequently talked about and debated *New Star* with their friends.

The power of television as an entertainment medium, a stimulator of political reflection, and a cultural reference point was clear as Chinese viewers watched, interpreted, and discussed *New Star*. By portraying one version of the reformation-in-action, the young institution of Chinese television had concretized, albeit fictionally, the abstract visions of progressive forces in China. *New Star*'s importance extends way beyond its appearance on the network airwaves. Television has played its most potent political role with this drama, stirring millions of Chinese citizens critically to analyze further their system of governance and to imagine possibilities for social change. Though the Chinese population is surely influenced by many sources other than television, the electronic medium diffuses its messages into the culture in a way that has no parallel. The reformation of China is inevitable. Programming that emanates from television sets so conspicuously present now in the homes of Chinese families will continue to be a crucial resource in the fulfillment of the nation's new visions, the construction of its very future.

This is an early draft of a chapter to be published in *China Turned On: Televisions, Reform and Resistance*, Routledge, forthcoming.

NOTES

1 I have developed this summary of *New Star* only after repeatedly viewing a videotape of the entire series with consultants from the People's Republic.
2 In the novel, however, this optimistic feeling sours when it is revealed that praise for Li given by the Province Secretary is the result of the prodding of his daughter, Shaoli. This detail is not made clear in the television series, but for readers of the novel this was a disturbing and disappointing development. It further indicated the *guanxi* problem. Shaoli's influence is not a good reason to praise Li or to support the concept of the reformation.
3 Most of the remainder of the sample also was not negative about *New Star*. Seven percent had no opinion while but 2 percent said they didn't like it.

REFERENCES

China Facts and Figures (1986) Beijing: Government Printing Office.
Dietrich, C. (1986) *People's China*, New York: Oxford University Press.
Gold, T. B. (1985) 'Personal relations in China since the Cultural Revolution', *China Quarterly* 104: 657–75.
Nathan, A. J. (1985) *Chinese Democracy*, New York: Alfred A. Knopf.
Pye, L. W. (1985) *Asian Power and Politics: Cultural Dimensions of Authority*, Cambridge, Mass.: Harvard University Press.
Wu, V-c. (1986) 'Some stories before and after *New Star* was produced: a chat with the *New Star* producer', *Shanghai TV Monthly* no. 49, July: 9–11.
Zhou, Y-p. (1986) 'The early morning "new star" – audience response investigation report about the television drama "*New Star*" ', in *Contemporary Literature and Art Thought*, Beijing: Government Printing Office.

7 Cultural variation in family television viewing

Cultures are not found, they are created socially. The family – variously constituted and culturally differentiated – is the interpersonal context in which much of this construction takes place, characteristically influenced by external and historical conditions (for instance, level of modernity, environmental factors, traditional values inherent in central considerations such as religion) and by idiosyncratic patterns of communication at home, including especially uses of language, styles of interpersonal interaction, and uses of mass media.

But we do not experience 'family' as an abstract sociological category. Each of us has a personal history with family that is invariably charged with emotion. Still, the family is something of an enigma for us since by the time we consciously realize what a family is, we already have one, and many of the attachments and dependencies that characterize life at home and help shape our personalities have already been formed. We enter the larger social world through the family, developing initial understandings of our own cultures by implicit reference to the lifestyle of people who live with us and who will, in most cases, be known to us for the rest of our lives.

The pervasiveness and importance of the family has stimulated a wide variety of research, theorizing, and criticism, especially since the turn of the last century with the birth of modern sociology. We can easily find scholarly accounts of the family that are written from a variety of theoretical perspectives and within many academic disciplines. But even the most recent accounts exclude consideration of the mass media, or treat them only as an aside, in their descriptions of family life. To media scholars this may seem to be an obvious oversight in need of correction. But media scholars have been guilty of the same crime from the other side of the issue.

Research on television has generally excluded in-depth treatment of the family – the natural viewing group. One cannot take 'the family' for granted. It must be treated as a problematic to be developed prominently in any attempt to theorize about the social and cultural significance of television.

DEFINING 'FAMILY'

Scholars are very careful now not to define 'family' as if there is a single or preferred type. Instead, there are 'families' of many varieties, even within national cultures, Generally, families are composed of persons who are related by blood or marriage, but not always. Sharing the same roof, food, dining table, money, material goods, or emotions could define any group as family.

Families in ethnically diverse countries are especially heterogeneous. In the United States, for instance, there are significant differences between and among families that are Asian-American, African-American, Latin-American, and European-American, even though members of all groups have a common sense of what it means to be an 'American family'. Immigrant families in their new lands differ in some ways from their kin in the old countries. Still, ethnic differences often persist in the form of values, and these values are present in the ways that families think and act. Socioeconomic classes within individual cultures are another critical determinant of difference, as is the number of persons in the living space, whether or not there are children present, and, when there are children, whether or not both parents live at home.

Despite all these complexities, the image that still often comes to mind when the term *family* is used is the *nuclear* or *conjugal* family – two parents and their dependent children, though for different reasons in various parts of the world, the group may not all live together. Another common form is the *extended* family, in which additional persons usually related by blood and marriage are part of the group. Members of the extended family may or may not live together, but they ordinarily maintain some emotional and material attachments. Families come in other forms, too, including descent groups, adoptive families, one-parent families, remarriage families, cohabitating units, and gay and lesbian families (Elliot 1986).

TELEVISION VIEWING AS FAMILY ACTIVITY

Family life embodies patterned social activities that are empirical representations of cultural values and understandings known as communication rules (Lull 1982a). These patterns are not homogeneous within cultures and there is always a fair amount of rule-breaking even within the most normative groups. Still, it is possible to identify many distinctive traits of family life in various world cultures by observing and comparing these regularities.

'Watching television' is a family activity that involves an intermeshing of the constantly changing personal agendas, moods, and emotional priorities of each family member with the fluctuating agenda of programs that emanates from TV sets. This does not mean that we cannot generalize about patterns – normative styles of viewing are evident in individual families and across families – but we must keep firmly in mind that these are highly complex and dynamic patterns. Further, television viewing is constructed by family members; it doesn't just happen. Viewers not only make their own interpretations of shows, they also construct the situations in which viewing takes place and the ways in which acts of viewing, and program content, are put to use at the time of viewing and in subsequent communications activity.

Television does not give families something to talk about, it directs their attention toward particular topics and, because families like to gather in front of the screen, the viewing situation is a convenient social setting in which to talk and otherwise communicate. Viewer *conversations* about program content are, in my view, one of the most powerful forms of empirical evidence to be considered in any substantive and revealing appraisal of the social and cultural aspects of television. *It is through talk about television that the audience is constituted in certain ways.* In his work on audience reception of television news, for instance, Jensen (1987) has identified what he calls 'super themes' – conversationally reconstructed descriptions of the content of newscasts. Sarett (1981) has shown how children verbally reproduce modified versions of television shows in the games they create during free time at school. Police officers construct work routines that incorporate the language and ideology of television police shows (Pacanowsky and Anderson, 1982). Young children enter adult conversations by referring to television themes as known-in-common cultural referents (Lull 1980).

Television programming presents constant images of social life,

including that of families, and is itself, therefore, an agent of socialization to role-differentiated behavior in families (Gunter and Svennevig 1987). The impact of television's incessant presentation of
social roles is sometimes a problem for cultures that differ in their
values from the places where these shows are produced. Ideas about
sex, romance, love, marriage, and family, for instance, are not the
same in the United States (the producer of most internationally
consumed shows) as they are in many other parts of the world.

FAMILY TELEVISION VIEWING RITUALS

It is easy to overlook the fact that Marshall McLuhan wrote his
most famous book, *Understanding Media* (1964), at a time when
television had been a part of everyday life in North America for
but slightly more than a decade. The subtitle of *Understanding
Media* is *The Extensions of Man*, and within that volume and in
later work McLuhan provided an insight that still has theoretical
currency. He claimed that mass media are *extensions* of human
perceptual senses – 'extensions of some human faculty – psychic or
physical' (McLuhan and Fiore 1967: 26).

I would like to suggest here that the involvements audience members have with television are indeed extensions of themselves, but
not just of their perceptual orientations or physical capabilities.
Audience members are family members, too, and their identities,
interests, and roles are articulated, acted upon, and played out in
routine activity at home. We can interpret much television viewing
as extensions of audience members' most basic and common mental
and behavioral orientations, nested and constructed within culturally diverse circumstances. For McLuhan, it is the mass media
themselves that extend the human senses by means of their technological capabilities. Here, the focus is on acts of viewing, wherein
audience members' interpretations and uses of television and video
cassette recorders extend not only the individual viewer, but also
social and cultural patterns and dispositions.

After conducting extensive ethnographic research in family homes
in the late 1970s, I published an article titled 'The Social Uses of
Television'. Empirical evidence I had collected in the field was
formulated into a typology reflecting family members' interpersonal
uses of both program content and the viewing experience itself. I
argued that television is a unique resource that family members
employ both during viewing and at other times to fulfill many
common desires and objectives at home. In practice, many social

uses of television are extensions of the personal and social positions and roles of family members, exercised normatively within their natural contexts, and constitutive of the most basic varieties and moments of family interaction. Now, I would like to organize many of the salient themes reported by contributors to *World Families Watch Television* (and some other data and ideas) into a multi-layered typology of audience 'extensions' that builds upon my previous empirical and theoretical work.

The framework for analysis employed here promotes a far more encompassing view of these activities than is typically recognized in audience research and theorizing, including my own social uses of television typology. The whole gestalt of the viewer's life situation figures into this theoretical schema. Processes of reception, interpretation, and use of television – the core of our empirical evidence – are recognized in the analysis. Cultural factors, social context, personalities of individuals, characteristics of the home environment, and the implications of technology, as they all contribute to the routine construction of family interaction, are central concerns here. Family life is analyzed with sensitivity to its characteristic diversity, contradictions, internal dynamics, and specific histories. The analysis reflects a *grounded theory* approach, wherein the empirical patterns and interpretive themes that emerge from the data are emphasized over programmatic interpretations that could be made according to a preconceived theoretical agenda.

THE CONSTRUCTION OF CULTURAL RITUALS

Many characteristic patterns of audience involvement with television can be regarded as *rituals* that are manifestations of microsocial (family) and macrosocial (cultural) *rules*. 'Ritual' refers to repeated, regular family activity, elevated to a near ceremonial level because of the cultural power of television. 'Rules' are socially co-ordinated understandings that promote patterned behavior, including routine acts of contact with the mass media (Lull 1982a). Social actors at least implicitly understand and employ rules in order to interact normatively.

I will frame much of the analysis according to the following principle: Life with television can best be understood by examining the rituals that individual family members and (often partial) families create at home. These rituals embody extensions of the normative values, mental orientations, and day-to-day behavior of individuals and families that are at least tacitly understood by everyone as rules of social interaction and communication. Rituals and under-lying rules are located in, influenced by, and definitive of some of the most central features of culture.

Audience extensions through television rituals

Let me make the analytical scheme clearer by beginning with an example of what I mean by 'extension': With written and photo-graphic documentation, Leoncio Barrios notes that the involvement children have with television in Venezuela is an extension of their play. Children bring their toys to the TV set and, in the process of arranging the toys around the set, include and define television. for themselves as a toy. In moments of play, they alternate their attention among all the toys, including television. Furthermore, television is not only an extension of children's playthings, *but an extension of their mental framework as well* – a desire for episodic or simultaneous attention given to several novel stimuli. Children integrate various aspects of their mental and material realities into a manageable sphere of entertainment, forming a consolidation of attractions. The ability of children to do their school homework in the presence of an activated and loud television set or stereo further exemplifies this integrative capacity of children. The integration may have additional, even contradictory, overlays. For many children, television viewing is also an extension of the *doing* of their school homework. Similarly, while viewing daytime soap operas may be an extension of the emotional interests of housewives, for instance, it can also be an extension of their housework.

EXTENSIONS AT THREE LEVELS OF ANALYSIS: THE CULTURE, THE HOUSEHOLD, THE PERSON

It is evident that the rituals of television use in the family adapt and amplify characteristics of the life situation at very different levels of specificity. Some aspects of television use interact with broad societal norms, while others primarily affect only the patterns of interaction within the family circle itself. Thus it is helpful to distinguish three levels of ritualized extension centered on tele-vision: the *culture*, characteristics of a social context broader than the family itself, the *household* (defined as the *domestic establish-ment*, including both family members and the physical location), and the *person*. Viewing activity, of course, does not divide neatly into these categories. In reality, much viewing is a simultaneous extension of the culture, the household, and the person. For analytical purposes, however, an inventory of the way television extends patterns of behavior will be presented in terms of this tripartite typology, and the supporting evidence of extensions will be related to these three levels of specificity. The discussion considers not only how audience members actively employ television to advance their family and individual interests, but also how television interacts with broader cultural values, conditions, and practices.

The final sections of the chapter are organized around central themes that have emerged from the contributed reports, particularly issues that concern gender and new technologies. In summarizing some of the central themes of the contributed reports, my own interpretations and comments have entered into the synthesis, at times taking a position in response to or elaborating upon the theoretical implications of these reports. I have attempted, however, to make clear points where my interpretations move beyond the accounts and interpretations provided by the contributors.

THE CULTURE

Cultural patterns are normative to the extent that they represent the fundamental *values*, *conditions*, and *practices* accepted by the whole society or by particular subcultural groups. While individuals or subcultural groups may resist aspects of the mainstream or dominant culture, the inherited overarching culture, demarcated in terms of national boundaries, language, and ethnicity, provides a basic framework of rules that guides the construction of everyday routines. For example, the way television is integrated into family routines will be influenced by and will reflect broader cultural themes of the society. At the same time, cultures are constantly changing, and societal norms permit areas of flexibility, growth, and further determination of norms, especially where new technologies, such as television, are being introduced. Within the over arching framework of culture, subgroups such as community and family are constantly extending and amplifying certain values, conditions, and practices through their own norm establishing action. This was apparent to Durre-Sameen Ahmed (1983), who has conducted a superb ethnography of family viewing in communal settings in Pakistan: 'The presence of TV and the ways it is used by the owners [of the TV sets] . . . intensify cultural patterns to an extent where they become more explicit and identifiable' (pp. 426–7). But as television is introduced or as the institution of television in a particular national context changes or is adapted through new technologies such as video, families will integrate television into their routines in ways that create new dimensions of existing values. It is not only the individual audience members who extend his or her personal or family interests, but, in so far as television is adopted throughout the society, the culture as a whole is transformed and extended.

Many cultural extensions are represented as main themes in the contributed reports. The reinforcement of the value of higher education which pervades the cultural policy for urban China and has deeper roots in Chinese culture can be seen not only in the official programming practices of the Chinese television system, but also in the preferences and characteristic interpretations of television by viewers. In India, social positions that have been defined by traditional religious norms and definitions of gender status are reproduced and amplified in viewing practices. In the more industrialized nations, television viewing extends the cultural trends toward family privatization. In Venezuela, the viewing of telenovelas, by far the most popular genre of television programming, reflects a cultural fascination with romantic melodrama and is a culture-based extension of female power (a theme that will be explored in detail later).

Cultural attitudes that are held by audiences toward the media themselves can be observed in styles of television viewing. In the report from West Germany, for instance, the critical orientation toward television held by people in much of Europe (increasingly present elsewhere, but *especially* in Europe) is apparent. In the European context, reading is widely considered to be superior to the use of television, a dominant cultural view that influences both media policy and viewer activity.

Telecommunications policy, television systems, and family viewing

The dialectic between the established cultural parameters of a society and the extension or modification of these parameters is especially evident in that part of the culture which is represented in the public media institutions. That is, the dominant social, cultural, and political values of a society have influenced many aspects of public media policy and organization of the media system. On the one hand, the policies with regard to number of hours of television transmission or the types of preferred programming, which may reflect political values emphasizing education or development, obviously limit the choices of television users. On the other hand, there is another logic operative in viewer preferences or in family routines that may run counter to the established policy and may deflect or transform the intended culturally and politically defined goal in an unintended way.

What is available for viewing, how much programming is transmitted, and when television stations operate is such an obvious set of influences that its interacting impact could be overlooked. The six countries represented in this chapter differ greatly in their telecommunications policies and systems. In most parts of India, for example, only one channel is available, while in the United States most viewers can receive at least ten or fifteen, and families with cable hookups are able to watch twenty, thirty or more channels in many metropolitan areas. The everyday routines of family members in most countries generally do not include much if any television viewing in certain parts of the day. None the less, a general trend in most countries is to increase the amount of television that is available by expanding the number of channels and extending the length of the broadcast day. As these changes are implemented, patterns of viewing and other routines at home also change.

The penetration of television into urban homes in all the countries reported herein, except for India, is nearly 100 percent. So, almost all urban viewers have *something* to view on television and people everywhere will watch television – that is constant across cultures. But the commitment to viewing and patterns of viewing are highly variable, depending in part on the availability and scheduling of shows.

Viewers often make a special effort to watch individual programs in situations in which few attractive shows are telecast. Low-abundance television settings also stimulate viewer configurations that differ from high-abundance contexts. Generally, we can say that when there are few good shows available, viewers watch them selectively and make more of a social activity out of viewing. There is less conflict over viewing choices, or over the decision whether or not to watch television at all, in situations in which there are so few attractive shows. This leads to a kind of cultural consensus on the desirability of viewing a particular show. During our research in China, for example, the Japanese soap opera *Oshin* was playing twice per week, and while many men claimed not to like the show very much, it would not have been reasonable for them to argue against family viewing.

The influence of a national broadcast system is not limited to the amount of time allotted to telecasting, the number of channels available, and scheduling, but also involves cultural values that are represented in programming. Television systems in various countries have their own principles for operation. There is always at least some official commitment to the idea that television should contribute to the well-being of society – that it should serve people's needs and be culturally uplifting, too. The major issue is what weight should be given to informational compared to entertainment programming. In those countries where the national government exercises great control over programming (for example, China, India, and West Germany, but also many other countries), there is invariably a mandate to present much informational programming. This is a priority in most developing countries because television can be used for education and technical training, literacy campaigns, distribution of health information, and presentation of international and domestic news, among other priorities.

But what audiences want mainly from television is not information, but *entertainment*. This is true in entertainment-saturated media environments like the United States and in entertainment-starved environments like China. Audiences everywhere list entertainment on television (especially drama and sports, but also children's programs, variety shows, films, and so on) as their favorite shows. It does not matter if it is a socialist or capitalist country, a system with many channels or just one, a more developed or less developed nation. So, while planners in some countries may in a sense try to force the informational capability of telecommunications on their viewers, the people will watch television for *their* purposes – entertainment.

Industrial and technological modernization

Television is introduced into the homes of families in different countries at different stages of national development with different impacts and meanings. There is a mixture of modernizing factors that influence the way television is accommodated into families in cultures around the world. These factors coinfluence family life. We must be careful when we examine family life in cities to consider national economic conditions, level of development or modernization, patterns of family migration, the loosening of kinship ties, housing conditions, modes of transportation, and how television – in its differing forms from country to country – interacts with all these factors to influence everyday life.

The roles and meanings of television in families also depend on levels of socioeconomic class within countries, not just on the overall level of national development. India offers such clear examples. For the urban elite in India, television now is just part of the mixture of modern appliances that surrounds them. For the poor, however, television assumes great importance, taking them from 'dark to light', providing new role models and restructuring some of the most basic everyday routines. Television can empower audience members, giving them access to information and entertainment they didn't have before – as is the case in India and China most recently. Ownership of a television set, especially a color model, is a source of status in these countries, too, just as it had been in the more developed countries years earlier.

Television in family space and time

The space in which families live has cultural significance that differs from country to country and from family to family within nations. Space refers to the amount of room, the way it is divided, what is placed where, and how things are used accordingly. For families that have much space, and more televisions, viewing need not distract others in the home since there is more domestic mobility. Consequently, there may be less conflict and friction since competing personal agendas and television program preferences can be worked out by moving to another part of the house. Families with a small amount of space, however, must use the room they have for many purposes, a spatial multifunctionality that is co-ordinated according to the demands of time and domestic priorities. These situations require on-going interpersonal negotiation and constant rearranging of furniture, scheduling of daily tasks, and adjustments of the mental orientations of family members. Viewing television under these circumstances is necessarily social most of the time.

The dividing up of space for television viewing also varies culturally. As is vividly described in the reports from India, the seating pattern for television viewing there is replete with meanings related to socioeconomic class and religious caste. But an interesting contradiction exists in the situation since all viewers share moments of viewing, including the emotional reactions and interpretations. This common focus and reception of entertainment in the private domain of the home is something new in India, and, as Neena Behl pointed out in her report, there are indications that at least intrafamilial status relations may be breaking down over this pattern of reception.

Cultures also have their own general sense of time, and there are tendencies to regulate social activity accordingly. Let me illustrate how cultural orientations toward time can influence family television viewing: Time means something very different in Denmark compared to Pakistan. In Denmark, nearly all families eat the evening meal at almost precisely the same time – 6:00 p.m. The evening television news is broadcast at 7:30, so that it won't interfere with dinner. The systematic, predictable pattern of the Danish orientation toward time, including the scheduling and viewing of television shows, is an extension of this very orderly culture. In Pakistan, on the other hand, television programs often appear on the state system at times that differ from the published schedules, or fail to appear at all. Audiences generally are not surprised or angered by these irregularities (Ahmed 1983). Cultural orientations that are held toward time necessarily encompass orientations that are held toward leisure time, and this in turn affects television viewing in different parts of the world.

But in the long run television also influences perceptions and uses of time within cultures that are very different. Mealtimes, bedtimes, choretimes, periods for doing school homework, and patterns of verbal interaction, among other activities, are influenced by the scheduling of television shows. Television is transforming the lives of some rural Indian families by changing their routines away from regulation by nature to regulation by the clock and by television. As Behl reported in her article, Sunday has become a 'TV holiday' and 'TV time' in the evening has replaced time that was previously used for transacting business and 'integrating thought' in rural Indian culture. The reports from India and China demonstrate another phenomenon that has occurred in all cultures with television – the speeding up of home activity, especially the preparation and consumption of the evening meal. Parts of the day become redefined and structured around the scheduling of TV shows, and certain behaviors (such as differing mealtimes for men and women in rural India) are consolidated in the interest of preserving time for viewing.

Staying home with television and video

A major trend in the western world apparent in the 1980s is that more and more families prefer to stay at home for their evening entertainment. In the United States, this phenomenon has been attributed to the fact that, among the 'baby boom generation' especially, in which more than 70 percent of the women work outside the home, both husband and wife are tired and prefer not to go out anywhere at night. Other reasons cited for the stay-at-home trend are the high cost of entertainment, a fear of violence, a lack of community involvement generally, and the easy availability of cable television and video. The phenomenon may signal a trend toward more conservative, traditional family lifestyles in the United States, Europe, and Great Britain, where 'home centeredness' is a contemporary social development. We cannot say that television has *caused* this phenomenon, but it has given families a substantial added reason to stay home. Television interacts with other factors – social, economic, and cultural – to create the stay-at-home trend. The predisposition to stay at home is encouraged by the ready availability of home entertainment. One result of the home-bound trend is the increased privatization of family life in the more developed countries such as Great Britain, West Germany, and the United States.

But families in China, India, and Venezuela are staying home with TV in the evenings now, too. The recreational attractiveness of television for families in these countries was discussed thoroughly in previous chapters. Certainly there is a novelty factor at work here, especially now in India. But some of the motivations for staying at home at night with television are the same in these countries as they are in North America and Europe. Another major reason for home-centeredness in Third World countries like China and India is the lack of transportation and the discomfort of the cinemas.

The celebration of holidays, family events, and other special occasions are cultural phenomena that now often take the form of social television viewing. According to Lu Weiping, a mass communication researcher in the People's Republic of China, viewing in *rural* China often takes place at the home of older couples since the families of their adult sons and daughters may not yet have television – a situation that is similar to early stages of adoption in the urban centers as well. Group television viewing now is part of the holiday celebration. According to Lu (1987):

An old woman told me that one Spring Festival's eve, many people went to her home to watch TV. The *kang* (a Chinese heatable brick bed, equal to the size of three double beds) was packed with viewers, and other people sat on little benches in front of the *kang*. That evening a vat of cold water (about 300 litres) was drunk by those visitors, and because there were so many of them, the hostess was unable to make tea for them . . . TV [is] a main part of Chinese recreational activities and it mirrors a close relationship among people in the rural area.

THE HOUSEHOLD

Family viewing takes place within the household, a complex mixture of people, social roles, power relations, routine activities, processes of interpersonal communication, ecological factors that characterize the home environment, and technological devices and appliances that exist there. The home surrounds viewers, and viewing, with all the intricacies and complications of family life.

The contributing authors have identified many situations in which the household is extended through the viewing practices of family members. Role-fulfilling activity such as mothers' interpretations of television for their children, for example, extends their customary domestic responsibilities for socialization and child care. British women's attention to local news and men's viewing of international television news and informational programming extends their contrasting modes of personal participation in public life and their specific and differing roles as family protectors and providers. Women in India arrange gatherings for the viewing of special television programs, extending their social and domestic roles. Women everywhere use television as a babysitter, extending role responsibilities for managing their children and for the simultaneous fulfillment of other domestic roles, another variety of extension. Some Indian men tease their women, comparing them to the starlets on television, extending their gender-based power in the marital relationship. Stay-at-home families that integrate television and video into their regular leisure-time activities extend the meaning of the home as an entertainment venue. The American 'TV dinner' (the practice, not the commercial product) extends the evening meal into a media setting.

Television viewing and talk about television are extensions of nearly all forms of interpersonal communication that take place between family members. Television is incorporated into strategies for avoiding or making physical or emotional contact with someone at home. Single-parent families may refer to the actions of TV characters in order to play out symbolically the role of the missing parent, thereby extending the family itself. Television is property, a piece of furniture that extends the decorative and material level of the family. Television is part of the media ensemble, and certain aspects of viewing are extensions of other media experiences. For instance, youth in India watch films on television in order to get visual referents for the music they hear on radio and audio cassette.

Economic circumstances within the home influence household activity and changes are reflected in television viewing. Jan-Uwe Rogge and Klaus Jensen from West Germany, and Dave Morley from England, for instance, have shown in their reports that unemployment has a dramatic effect on styles of family viewing – the amount of viewing that is done, what is viewed and what it means, and how it fits in with the other family activity. For unemployed men, television may serve as an escape, a compensation, or a 'regression' (to use Rogge and Jensen's term). And, according to Morley, emotional relationships and communication between husbands and wives also change in conditions of male unemployment as new viewing patterns are negotiated at home. Television viewing patterns are intimately bound up with social relations at home, and both these considerations are influenced by matters such as employment status or changes in the composition of family membership, as was described in the report from Germany.

THE PERSON

While the analysis that is made in this chapter is framed primarily in terms of the culture and the family, it is also apparent that personality attributes, mental orientations, and specific activities of the person, the individual viewer, are extended in routine acts of television viewing. Moreover, while we study the family as a unit or system, we still must take into account the often competing interests and agendas of individuals in families. For research purposes, then, 'the family' can be taken as a unit of analysis, but we must realize that families do not act as complete and harmonious groups in most of their television viewing. Whether one is male or female, for instance, predicts differences in preferences for television programs and styles of viewing, important themes that will be taken up at length in a subsequent section of this chapter.

Contrasts in viewing done by people of different age groups reveal types of personal extension, too. In China, for instance, members of the older generation repeatedly watch televised Chinese operas, extending their age-based identities according to nostalgic cultural associations and pleasures. Younger viewers prefer the more modern stories. The curiosity that viewers have about life in other lands motivates them to watch television for exposure to these exotic locations, a McLuhanesque-type extension of the senses. Use of television to fulfill emotional desires or to compensate for emotional disturbances are extensions of affective conditions into viewing practices. The interests and activities of individual viewers are also extended into television viewing, as was shown in the example given of children's incorporation of television into their play.

Among the attributes of the person that are extended through viewing, then, are age, generation, gender, sexual orientation, and personality. Mental orientations include emotions, fantasies, moods, pleasures, fears, personal interests and identities, vocational and professional interests, compensations, processes of discovery and reality exploration, personal reinforcement, and the desire for companionship (parasocial interaction). Individual activities include relaxing, passing time, escaping, isolating to maximize emotional involvement, changing moods, and simple exposure to entertainment as a leisure-time attraction.

In the next sections of this chapter I will elaborate on some of the central issues that have been raised in the ethnographic reports and in the analysis provided above. I will pay special attention to gender-based matters as these have become focal concerns in the research.

FAVORITE TELEVISION SHOWS OF MEN AND WOMEN

Differences in program preferences held by men and women all over the world follow a predictable pattern. These differences do not depend on the type of political-economic system of individual nations or on specific television programming policies within the countries. Men everywhere prefer sports, action-oriented programs, and information programming (especially news), while women prefer dramas (including serials, soap operas, and films) and music/-dance/comedy-based programs.

Differing program preferences held by males and females have been researched directly by Dave Morley. In England, women are especially fond of love stories and experience these shows as 'guilty pleasures', according to Morley. The 'daily weepies' are favorites of women in West Germany, too. We looked into this issue in China as well and were intrigued to find that the program preferences we have in the west coincide almost perfectly with program preferences held by men and women viewers in China. We see the same pat-

terns in Venezuela, especially with the female audience for telenovelas, and in India, where, according to Behl's observations of
the rural scene, women walk away from the set when 'discussions'
appear, preferring dance, music, serials, and films. News, documen-
taries, and other factually based programs are frequently watched
by males in all these cultures. Men express the greatest interest
and emotional involvement, however, for sports programming, and,
to a lesser degree, for action programs.

These characteristic differences between men and women appear
not to be bound by culture or by time. In a study done in the early
days of television in the United States, for example, Gans (1962)
found that working-class Italian-American men preferred sports and
action-oriented drama. Gans noted that these programs minimize
dialogue and provide a flow of masculine images that, according to
the author, permit the viewer to live his life vicariously the way he
would like to in the real world. Women, according to Gans, prefer
programs that are 'just the opposite. They like musical programs,
soap operas, and other stories that deal with romance or with family
situations and problems, even middle-class ones. Men who choose
stories that are popular with women are classified as sissies. One
"West Ender" (the part of Boston where Gans did his research)
was accused of "going soft" and becoming "half woman" because
he was not interested in watching sporting events' (Gans 1962: 188).

To borrow a term from Cees Hamelink (1983; he was using
the term to describe the worldwide production of programs, not
reception), we find a certain 'cultural synchronicity' in the program
preferences held by people from these disparate places. We cannot
explain patterns of program preference as logical consequences of
specific cultural circumstances, since the same patterns appear in
cultures that are extremely diverse in every respect. Why is it that
men and women from such different cultures have such predictable
program preferences?

At first, differences in program preference between males and
females seem distinct. However, there may be a false dichotomy
present between the apparent factual interests of men and the
fictional interests of women. While sports programs are factual –
there is no script for the playing and outcome of sports events –
games and matches are not just informational events. They are
stories, too. They provoke emotional reactions. A good game, like
good stories of all kinds, is a drama, full of suspense and surprises.
You don't know the ending until the last scene – the final few
minutes of the game. And, there are layers of public discourse that

surround sports stars, just like the celebration of other popular culture heroes, that add even more flair to the drama.

News is dramatic, too. After all, news items are called 'news stories', and in commercially competitive nations like the United States, consultants commonly urge television stations to make their news stories more dramatic in order to win viewers. So, while men and women prefer different types of television shows, extending their gender identities and social roles into characteristic viewing patterns, ultimately they may be expressing preference for *a type of story* rather than for programming that at first appears to be completely different.

VIEWING STYLES OF WOMEN AND MEN

Dave Morley (1986) has analyzed family life with television from a perspective that compares the domestic activities of women and men. He concludes that males assert cultural power within the realm of domestic relations, including the construction of routine acts of television viewing. Morley's insightful work is framed within a feminist interpretation of domestic relations in England, focusing on an extension of male power in the context of working-class households.

A summary of the differences in viewing styles between men and women in England can be described thus: Men plan their viewing carefully, watch television attentively, watch 'wholeheartedly', and are able to relax with television. Home is a 'site of leisure' for employed men, a place they can relax when the work day is done. Men focus on their preferred shows more. They also control the technical aspects of television, including the remote control device, which they may use for unnegotiated channel switching, thereby asserting their preferences and wielding 'cultural power' even more.

Women, on the other hand, do not have as much say as men in the selection of shows or in possession and use of the technical aspects. They watch television far less attentively (more 'distract-edly') because they are constantly trying to manage their domestic responsibilities in addition to whatever viewing they can do at night. They are forced to construct other times for viewing, during the day for instance, when they can watch television with less distractions. Home is a 'site of work' for women, so they can never truly relax and enjoy viewing in the more fulfilling way that men do.

This gender-based interpretation certainly has an internal logic and explanatory value. But there are some questions that emerge from this work that require additional evidence and interpretation. Fundamentally, I want to provide additional perspectives on three considerations that emerge from Morley's work: the nature of attention, the variability of viewing pleasure, and the significance of cultural context.

Attention to television

The notion of 'attentive viewing' is posed by Morley as a nonproblematic and favorable condition. But *attention* is very much a relative concept, since there is no such thing as full attention to the screen. Viewers watch television only with relative amounts of attention. And how do you measure attention in the first place? Looking at the screen certainly does not mean that the viewer is giving full attention, and viewers do not constantly look at the screen anyway. Several studies that have employed television cameras to document viewer behavior clearly show that there is much movement and activity around the television set, and that the amount of viewer eye contact with the screen is highly variable and not sustained for long periods of time in any case. There is a wide range of activities that accompany viewing.

The most recent work along these lines further shows that viewers who spend the *most* time in front of the set look at the screen far *less* proportionately than viewers who are in and out of the room (Collett 1986). Unfortunately, Collett does not account for male/-female differences in his report of British viewing activity. He claims that the viewing experience is generally busy, interrupted by many other activities, and routinely accompanied by talk, much of it having nothing to do with the program. Collett's observations were made in both upper-middle-class and working-class families. It is difficult to draw strong conclusions about patterns of attention since the samples in both the Morley and Collett researches were small, and, because of Collett's mixed sample and failure to discuss male/-female differences, we don't exactly know how his data differs from what Morley describes. The actual nature of 'attention to the screen' in family viewing requires additional study, and must be considered in relation to 'modes of viewing' as well as to presentational practices of television systems throughout the world. The situation in the United States, for instance, differs greatly from Europe. The frequent appearance of commercial announcements in America may stimulate discontinuous viewing patterns that are far less 'distracted' than is the case elsewhere.

Tom Lindlof and his American colleagues have made a useful distinction between viewing modes, each of which portends a different viewing style. There is not only relatively *focused* viewing, according to these researchers, but also *monitoring*, where television viewing is secondary to some other primary activity. Viewers in this mode watch television just enough to keep up with what is happening on the show. A third category they describe is *idling*, where viewer involvement with television is low, since the person is just passing time between other activities and 'watching' television is but a momentary distraction. Patterns of attention, therefore, must be considered in relation to modes of viewing.

Commercial advertisers in the United States – people who have a lot at stake over the issue – know much about how viewers watch TV. They assume that viewers are *not* paying attention and that they must constantly try to capture and hold their interest. For this reason, commercials are full of devices that are designed to attract viewers' attention again and again. Attention to the screen cannot be assumed for any viewer.

Viewing pleasure

I would like to consider 'attention' in relation to viewing pleasure, and then to discuss various sorts of viewing pleasures. As Morley states, staring at the television set can mean everything from 'total fascination' to 'boredom'. If a person is 'attentive' but bored, is this a positive viewing experience? This raises the interesting possibility that viewers who are monitoring television while engaged in another primary activity may be enjoying the experience as much as others who sit there with their eyes fixed on the screen (that certainly is how I feel about viewing. I have *never* been able to enjoy television viewing as a sole activity). Making television viewing the primary activity also does not necessarily mean that more thought is given to the program than would be the case in the monitoring mode. The monitoring viewer may actually be more alert to developments in the program, while the 'focused' viewer may be daydreaming about something else entirely. Viewing as a primary activity, therefore, does not necessarily mean that the experience is more pleasurable. In fact, peripheral viewing styles may be more involving and more pleasurable. In her writing about women's viewing practices, for instance, Modleski is of the opinion that in their characteristic 'distracted' viewing mode, 'the flow of various programs and commercials tend to make repetition, interruption, and distraction pleasurable' (Modleski 1982: 102). At least it seems fair to conclude that different modes of viewing produce pleasures of different sorts, and that any attempt to evaluate and compare these pleasures in the empirical realm is immediately problematic.

Also, of course, many women do engage in relatively more focused viewing of certain programs, especially dramatic presentations, including soap operas and serials, at other times of the day. Many housewives and housekeepers find time during the day to watch their favorite shows. They are often able to establish a private viewing environment to promote the kind of pleasure that this type of programming can provide, a very emotional experience, apparently. So the family viewing mode at night is, for many women, but one style of viewing in which they engage. Survey statistics show that women watch much more television than men do and that women all over the world have more access than men to television during the daytime. *Different types of programs elicit different styles of viewing for different people at different times of the day.*

The male viewing mode is similarly complex and insufficiently explained so far. The best work in this area is clearly Morley's, and his analysis is limited to British working-class men. Supposedly men have privileged status in the family viewing situation. But what actually happens?

First, men are regular viewers of television news at night, often turning the set on when they get home in order to be sure to see it. It may be enjoyable for them to do so, but it also signals a commitment to the responsibility for gaining information that is useful to the well-being of the family. Watching television news has instrumental value for them. Second, when fathers arrive home after work, there is a characteristic shifting of the attention of children in the house away from whatever they are doing, and away from their mother toward their father. Fathers, therefore, often assume great emotional responsibility for the children at night, and this fatherly role continues into evening television viewing. Fathers, therefore, may be distracted emotionally by their children during the evening while mothers are preoccupied more with chores related to supervising their activities.

Even in families in which both parents work, males typically are the full-time 'breadwinners', a family role that has unparalleled emotional demands. The stresses of their work are commonly taken home by men, and, accustomed as they are to take this bottom-line responsibility for their families, they cannot simply 'turn off' their thinking about work, even by watching television, although they may mightily try to do so. My point is that men also are working while they watch television – assuming an emotional and often physical involvement with their children, thinking about work, making plans, but also doing other 'responsible' things like reading the newspaper or performing household tasks. The work that men do at home may simply be less observable or less commonly categorized as 'work'. Much of men's viewing, therefore, is actually something other than what it appears to be or is described to be – even by men.

The cultural context

The analytical details debated above are really minor compared to the influence that varying cultures have in terms of how men and women negotiate and view television programs. The discussion above pertains mainly to family life in the more developed countries. In China, for instance, we did not find the variety of male dominance in family television viewing that Morley reports from England or that I have found in some of my own research in the United States (Lull 1982b). The reports from India also indicate that while men may have more *formal* say than women in program selection, women may exercise greater *actual* influence. But the best example of cultural variability is the case of Venezuela.

In Venezuela, the television set is an extension of the domestic environment, and women control the domestic environment. There is no male head of the household in about half the homes in Venezuela. Naturally, women manage family activity in these single-parent homes, but this cultural trait sends a strong cue that influences the domestic personality of intact nuclear families as well. Furthermore, the 'home' and patterns of family members leaving and returning home every day are typically very different in Venezuela compared to England, the United States, or West Germany, for instance. The marital relationship is subsumed within these cultural orientations.

The work that women do at home in Venezuela is generally shared among members of the extended family in poor families or by hired help in families of the middle and upper classes. Women who work outside the home rarely come home to responsibilities for preparation of the evening meal or child care. The home may be a 'site of work' for women in Venezuela, but it is not its dominant meaning and the work is undertaken collectively in any case. For Venezuelan women, the home is where their beloved children are, where they feel secure, and where they exercise their cultural power. Men respect women's 'right of decision' in the home. Although men surely have more power than women in the public sphere, women have great control over the emotional atmosphere and the agenda of activity in the household.

Recognizing this, the television networks and stations put programs (the telenovelas) on at night especially for the female audience. At one point programmers attempted to put male-oriented programs on during this time, but the shows were miserable failures in the ratings since women, who control night-time viewing, were watching the telenovelas on the other channels. More than 80 percent of the television audience watches telenovelas during evening prime time.

Television viewing in Venezuela has a feminine quality to it. Programs are chosen by women and are generally watched under circumstances dictated by them. Watching telenovelas is not within the acceptable range of *machismo* behavior, so men must not watch, watch out of the corner of their eyes, or watch something else on another set if one is available and something else is on. Women regularly talk about the telenovelas with their friends (indeed, it is a *major* topic in conversation for them) while men do not talk about these shows. This is similar to our finding in China, where men talk excitedly about sports programs with their friends at work, but rarely admit to watching drama serials, and certainly don't discuss the stories with their friends.[1]

Not only does the telenovela reign supreme on Venezuelan television, only certain kinds of soap operas gain popularity. These are shows that celebrate the emotional preferences of Venezuelan women – love and romance. American-style serials that feature power and money (like *Dallas*) do not resonate well with Venezuelan culture or draw large audiences comparable to the local dramatic productions.

THE VIDEO CASSETTE RECORDER, GENDER, AND FAMILY ROUTINES

Over-the-air television is but one way to receive programs at home, and in the more developed countries it is steadily losing its monopoly on viewing practices. The two major competitors are cable television and the video cassette. Cable is a complicated communications technology, requiring an expensive and cumbersome delivery system. While about half the homes in the United States are hooked up to the cable, the penetration of cable in Germany is only about 20 percent now and England is 'cabled' to less than 5 percent. China, India, and Venezuela do not have cable systems. The more accessible medium is the video cassette recorder (VCR). Statistics representing family ownership are climbing rapidly in many parts of the world. For families with VCRs, the machine becomes part of the 'media ensemble', requiring families to adapt and construct a new 'media world', where the new option is incorporated into existing patterns of media activity and into daily life generally.

We are in the early stages of documenting and understanding the social and cultural meanings of the video cassette recorder. The introduction of the VCR into the home certainly requires an adjustment in family patterns – an 'accommodation' to use Lindlof's term. The VCR requires a rethinking of family viewing since it becomes a competitor for over-the-air and cable television. It even uses part of the previous medium's hardware, the screen, thereby preventing the viewing of regular programming at the same time on that set – the main set in most cases. The family constructs new patterns of viewing – of video and television – that may also require the articulation of new rules for access. This is especially the case in families with children since they are most likely to have a VCR (Gunter and Svennevig 1987). The addition of a VCR at home increases the entertainment options, provides more control over viewing (thereby changing the viewing experience for audiences) and makes the interpersonal dynamics of the home more complex.

The VCR may be further widening the 'gender gap' between men and women at home, as the reports from the United States, England, and West Germany indicate. As Rogge and Jensen point out, some women even believe that the new media symbolize underdeveloped human relations and a decline in interpersonal communication at home. The German authors refer to the world of new media as a 'masculine domain'. The VCR is a logical extension of the masculine roles of installing and operating home equipment. Men are usually responsible for these pieces of equipment. They are the family members who develop user competency. Many new technologies – especially the entertainment media – are 'toys' for men, and they enjoy playing with them. So, the responsibility becomes a kind of male pleasure. The operation of some of this equipment also is a function that men are expected to perform for their families. The responsibilities, pleasures, and functions that men have with these pieces of equipment give them some degree of control over them and over other family members along the way.

Previous research has shown that in the United States and England, at least, men have greater say than women over the selection of television programs that are viewed by families at night. This pattern appears to be reflected again in the uses that are made of the VCR, according to the authors from the United States, England, and West Germany. This typical male control of the VCR as an extension of their roles played out within the 'masculine domain' raises an interesting question about viewing for nuclear families in places like Venezuela, where, so far at least, family television viewing is more an extension of the domestic power of women.

There are also indications that children of both sexes develop competency with VCRs, home computers, compact disc players, and other entertainment media. And in rural India, according to Behl, this competency also extends into other areas of new domestic equipment. Children's natural curiosity and their desire to take advantage of these machines stimulates their learning how to operate them. Accommodation of new entertainment technologies into the home, therefore, may be influenced as much by generation as it is by gender, at least in certain cultural settings.

Other implications of the VCR for families

(a) Watching something on the VCR, especially a rented or purchased video, has greater status as a viewing event than does regular television. This has many connotations, including who is responsible for choosing the material to be played, how it will be paid for, when it will be played, and how it will be integrated into television viewing and the use of other media.

(b) The special status that playing a video has often makes the event more social. Arranging the social dimension of the playback may become a responsibility of women at home, while selection of the video and operation of the machine is more likely to be done by men.

(c) Viewing need not take place in real time. Viewers regulate the flow of imagery, starting and stopping the machine for any number of reasons. This management of time requires interpersonal co-ordination and offers new potentials and problems for family viewing. The stress of reported 'distracted' styles of viewing, for instance, could be reduced by watching video since the program can be stopped while household tasks are performed. On the other hand, to *not* stop the machine during these moments could elevate the stress since control of the flow of programming is in the hands of audiences and to disregard another viewer is a strong negative statement.

(d) The possibility for 'repeated viewing' brings video into a status that is similar to other art forms, such as paintings, records, audio tapes, books, and poetry, that are typically appreciated more than once by audiences. Families that can afford to buy videos are doing so in great numbers, building video libraries and watching the shows multiple times. Each viewing is a different kind of experience. Since the story is known after the first viewing, audiences presumably focus more on specific scenes and lines of dialogue during subsequent viewings, experiencing the same program in a different way each time. Any film buff recognizes this pattern. The VCR has extended this manner of viewing to a wide audience.

(e) Unlike television, the VCR permits ownership of programs in the form of videotapes. These tapes can be displayed in the house like books or magazines to project an image of the owner to family members and others – a social use of the new medium and an extension of the audience member.

(f) The technical capabilities of the VCR – especially the 'fast forward' option – permit a user-controlled tempo of viewing. Many viewers speed up the video during 'boring' parts. The effect may be a kind of 'viewer impatience' that may even be taken into consideration by producers and directors of videos and film. And, as has been pointed out by Morley, whoever controls the VCR remote control device may wield disproportionate influence over matters such as these.

CONCLUDING REMARKS

At the beginning of this chapter I developed a framework for analysis of family television viewing around the world by describing extensions of viewers at the cultural, household, and personal levels. The contributing authors have each presented empirical accounts that encouraged formulation of a theoretical perspective on 'extension' that goes beyond McLuhan's original 'extension of the senses' argument. The resulting typology surely does not cover all the empirical possibilities, but it organizes and synthesizes the findings and interpretations.

Within the perspective of extensions, family members are considered to be active constructors of their everyday lives. Television is not only a technological medium that transmits bits of information from impersonal institutions to anonymous audiences, it is a social medium, too – a means by which audience members communicate and construct strategies to achieve a wide range of personal and social objectives. The contributed reports in this volume provide much evidence in support of this vision. But the cultural, social, and personal implications of television are not just the result of intentional enactments performed by television viewers. As McLuhan himself asserted, there is a large-scale impact resulting from the involvements that audiences have with mass media – 'effect' is a term he often used. Implicitly framed within his writing is a fundamental issue that still must be taken into account in the development of mass communication theory: simultaneous consideration of the willing involvement that audience members have with television and other media together with attention to the technological and ideological power and impact of the media – a theoretical opposition of uses and effects.

It is clear that audience members do not live in a 'free field' at home or anywhere else, uninfluenced by textual and technological factors and the ideological agenda and force they contain and impose. However, viewers also are not 'constructed by the text', nor are their experiences 'determined' by the technological, economic, or ideological structures that are associated with mass media. Television viewing in family settings throughout the world occurs along the lines of cultural, household, and personal extensions of audience members that represent the interests of viewers but are also influenced by factors external and internal to the home that are not under their control. The concept of extension, therefore, is both dynamic and dialectical, incorporating the reproduction of cultural, household, and personal agendas, but constantly embodying change stimulated by influences that are introduced to the culture, the household, and the person. The ceaseless negotiations taking place at all three levels of specificity identified here give a clue to the inescapable conclusion that while certain homogenizing tendencies of television and video appear throughout the world, world families also watch television distinctively within their own cultures.

This chapter was originally published in *World Families Watch Television*, Sage Publications, 1988.

NOTES

1 The exceptions are docudramas or stories that have special relevance to men. For instance, the 12-part drama series *Xin Xing* (*New Star*), a highly controversial program about political reform in China that had appeared on the national system a few months before we conducted our study there, was watched and talked about enthusiastically by men.

REFERENCES

Ahmed, D. S. (1983) 'Television in Pakistan: an ethnographic study', doctoral dissertation, Columbia University.

Collett, P. (1986) 'Watching the TV audience', paper presented to the International Television Studies Conference, London.

Elliot, F. R. (1986) *The Family: Change or Continuity?*, Atlantic Highlands, NJ: Humanities Press International.

Gans, H. (1962) *The Urban Villagers*, New York: Free Press.

Gunter, B. and Svennevig, M. (1987) *Behind and in Front of the Screen: Television's Involvement with Family Life*, London: John Libbey.

Hamelink, C. (1983) *Cultural Autonomy in Global Communications*, New York: Longman.

Jensen, K. B. (1987) 'The social uses of news: a qualitative empirical approach to the reception of television news', paper presented to the International Communication Association, Montreal.

Lu, W. (1987) Personal correspondence, Department of Sociology, Beijing University, People's Republic of China.

Lull, J. (1980) 'The social uses of television', *Human Communication Research* 6, 3: 197–209.

—— (1982a) 'A rules approach to the study of television and society', *Human Communication Research* 9, 1: 3–16.

—— (1982b) 'How families select television programs: a mass observational approach', *Journal of Broadcasting* 26, 4: 801–11.

McLuhan, M. (1964) *Understanding Media: The Extensions of Man*, New York: McGraw-Hill.

—— and Fiore, Q. (1967) *The Medium is the Message*, New York: Bantam.

Modleski, T. (1982) *Loving with a Vengeance*, New York: Methuen.

Morley, D. (1986) *Family Television: Cultural Power and Domestic Leisure*, London: Comedia.

Pacanowsky, M. and Anderson, J. A. (1982) 'Cop talk and media use', *Journal of Broadcasting* 26, 4: 757–81.

Sarett, C. (1981) 'Socialization patterns and preschool children's television and film-related play behavior', doctoral dissertation, University of Pennsylvania.

8 Ethnographic studies of broadcast media audiences: notes on method

Despite the fact that most media consumption occurs at home, little social research on broadcasting has been conducted there. The family home is an intimate location. Particularly in this country, where emphasis is placed on privacy, the idea of invading the home to do social research does not appeal to most researchers. To date, naturalistic studies of families have been rare. Naturalistic studies of broadcast audiences conducted in homes are even less common.

There are some exceptions. An observational study of seventeen 'normal' and disturbed families were undertaken by two Boston psychiatrists and their associates (Kantor and Lehr 1975). Henry wrote about five psychiatrically disturbed families after living with each for one week (Henry 1965). Lewis lived with Mexican and Puerto Rican families, observed their activities in relation to their histories, interviewed them, and reconstructed their realities in his written accounts (Lewis 1959, 1965).

The famous videotaped ethnography of the William Loud family was aired on public television. More recently, Wilkes documented the lives of *Six American Families* for public television. He also wrote a short book about these families and the method he used (Wilkes 1977). I have developed a typology of the social uses of television by living with families and documenting their communication habits (Lull 1980a). Reid provided a symbolic interactionist interpretation of children's time spent watching television commercials using observations collected in homes (Reid 1979). Other researchers have also begun to collect ethnographic data on media audiences (Meyer *et al.* 1980). Naturalistic studies of audience behavior probably will be undertaken more frequently in the future.

This essay provides specific methodological suggestions for researchers who intend to conduct observational studies of broadcast audiences. Data also are presented regarding the effect of the observer on the family unit, with special attention to potential disturbances of family television viewing.

METHODOLOGICAL ISSUES

The ethnographer of family audience behavior must be concerned with: (1) sampling, (2) observational techniques, (3) stages of data collection, and (4) organizing and presenting data. This discussion focuses on lessons learned from research conducted during the past several years in Wisconsin and California, where observations and interviews of more than 300 families have been made for periods of three to seven days each.

Sampling

Depending on the number of families required, the sampling can be very time consuming and frustrating. None the less, as many as ninety observers have been placed simultaneously in families previously unknown to them (Lull 1980b). Through trial and error, an effective means has been found for locating families who will permit extended observations in their homes.

Random phone calls or neighborhood surveys conducted to contact families initially have not worked well. Even the most conservatively dressed representative with the most apparently benign intent has been unable to convince subjects to open their doors for observation. Contact through some agency of importance to the family is usually necessary to gain access. These agencies include religious and educational institutions, places of work, community service groups, and clubs. If the agency is of great importance to the family (as in the case of religious or vocational institutions), then families in the sample are likely to be homogeneous.

Civic groups and clubs represent a wider range of family types. Even though there may be less emotional commitment to these organizations when compared with religious or vocational groups, most families still honor a basic commitment to community groups and respect the desires of their leaders, thereby increasing the likelihood that they will agree to participate. Groups such as girls' clubs, boys' clubs, Parent Teacher Associations, and community nursery schools have been especially cooperative. Some family research requires that children of a particular age be present in the home, and these agencies can be helpful.

A successful approach to gaining groups' cooperation has been first to call their administrators, explaining the essential nature of the research program and requesting to address the next board meeting. At the board meeting, the general nature of the research project is explained, and the cooperation of the group is requested. The researcher's affiliation with a local university and the noncommercial nature of the investigation are persuasive factors. The researcher describes an interest in studying 'communication in families' or 'family life' (never mentioning mass communication or television viewing).

The executive group is asked to endorse the research project and to provide access to telephone lists of their members or to allow a personal appeal for volunteer subjects at the next meeting of the general membership. Telephone calls, in which the research project is identified as being conducted cooperatively with the group, have been more productive of willing families than have been speeches to the general membership of these community groups. Both approaches have been effective, however. Depending on the project and the group, 25–35 percent of the families contacted initially have been willing to participate.

From families that agree to serve as subjects, an additional 10–20 percent will not provide usable data for various reasons. Oversampling is necessary for studies that involve many observers and families. No effort has yet been made to determine whether the kinds of families who self-select into samples for ethnographic studies are different from those who do not cooperate. Sampling procedures have generated an assortment of family types. Whether this assortment is representative of American families overall is a methodological consideration that has not been investigated.

Families have not been paid when students do the observing and when the length of time involved is short. When inconvenience to the family is great, as in week-long stays, families have been paid a small amount of money and asked to provide food. Arrangements have sometimes been made, particularly with farm families, for the observers to perform certain work tasks in order to compensate for the inconvenience they may cause.[1] Observers have not always slept at subjects' homes. Little data seem to be lost if the researcher leaves at bedtime and returns the next morning.

Observational techniques

The particular theoretical and conceptual concerns that motivate a research project determine what qualifies as observational evidence and what the manner for documentation of family data should be. Naturalistic studies in communication, such as those that analyze conversational form, may require precise documentation of verbal interaction. Audio- and videotape recorders have sometimes been used to document conversations, but this technique has rarely been used in home settings.

The use of electronic recording equipment to study family television viewing has been tried at least once but with limited success. In a study by Bechtel and his associates, television cameras were placed on top of the television sets of a small sample of families in order to document their behaviors while viewing (Bechtel *et al.* 1972). Microphones were placed around the room in order to record conversations and personal reactions to the shows. The scope of this research project was limited only to the characteristics of eye contact, physical movement, and talk patterns while viewing. These are interesting considerations, but the ethnographer usually wants to learn more about the environment in which these behaviors are taking place.

It is technically possible to pin small cordless microphones on each family member while a slow speed, multitrack audiotape recorder documents everything said during the observational period (one track on the recording unit assigned to each person). The difficulties with this approach are that the equipment is expensive and the researcher has no record of where the taped comments were made. This latter problem can be overcome by continual note-taking by the observer. In spite of the problems, such a technical device may prove to be suited to studying family life.

Currently, the most effective method for documenting the activities of family life is still written notes made by the observer. Note-taking in the presence of families is an awkward task that must be done in a way that attracts minimum attention. Student observers may have an advantage since they can take notes in the guise of homework chores. This technique has often worked well in the study of media audience behavior, since many families spend their evenings in front of the television set. The student observer, also seated in the viewing area but surrounded by homework, can easily take notes on interpersonal interaction that accompanies viewing. It is helpful to document conversations as they unfold, a goal facilitated by taking notes in this fashion.

The natural breaks occurring during observational studies give the researcher time to take detailed notes about what transpired during the preceding minutes or hours. Reconstruction of the scene is more accurately accomplished when opportunities are created to take notes during the actual observational period. Additional notes can be made at bedtime. At first, many families are sensitive to observer note-taking, and it is sometimes difficult to be unobtrusive during early stages of the research. Note-taking becomes less troublesome during later stages of data collection.

Stages of data collection

An ethnographer studying family life at home must first decide the length of the observational period for each family. The time unit must be sufficiently long to understand the family and to insure that the behaviors observed are not staged for the researcher's benefit, thereby obscuring valid identification of concepts and relationships. On the other hand, observation should cease when the important characteristics of social structure and process have been identified and documented. Seven days is often an excellent time, for reasons that will be discussed later. At least three days per family seems to be the minimum.

It is necessary to establish rapport with family members sufficient to insure the gathering of valid self-reports and accounts by subjects of the perceived attitudes and behaviors of others. The privacy of the home and the small number of subjects involved in family research may make the observer's presence more conspicuous than in other settings. None the less, the observer who is accepted into the family system can provide 'camera-like views of the movements, conversations and interactions' in a way no other social research method can rival (Lewis 1959: xxii).

When researchers live in the homes of families, 'stages of familiarity' or 'stages of trust' develop. These stages vary from observer to observer and from family to family, but some basic techniques can help standardize the sequence of events and the time they require.

The process typically develops in three stages. In the first stage, spanning roughly the first two days of observation, family histories, biographical sketches, and descriptions of the physical environment are the primary elements recorded. Time can be spent effectively noting everyday objects, such as home furnishings, clothing, ornaments, tools, domestic appliances (particularly the location of television and radio receivers), and other equipment (Madge 1953). This is a natural and convenient development since the researcher immediately encounters the physical aspects of the environment when the observational period begins. It is perhaps best to document these items right away anyway, since their appearance may be more striking at first than later, when the researcher has become accustomed to the surroundings.

Families often begin to reveal much of their past and present during the first day or two of observation. This revealing of personal information is often produced with little or no stimulation and makes the situation more relaxed. The researcher may feel more comfortable by saying something personal at this time, although specific references to the objectives of the research program should not be made.

Interaction sequences, family routines, communication habits, particular media uses, and more detailed personal information become accessible to the researcher during the second stage of the research. Using a seven-day model for the period of observation, the second stage typically begins late in the second day or during the third day. The researcher begins to feel that the interpersonal dramas unfolding are normal.

During this second stage, the observer must create and sustain rapport with family members while maintaining the disinterested eye and ear of the objective observer-reporter. He or she must also understand each family member's acts from the actor's perspective while retaining an objective attitude toward the 'actor and the action scene' (Cicourel 1974: 50). The close quarters of family studies can make the adjustment of the observer to the subjects, and their adjustment to him or her, difficult. The observer must engage in enough conversation and physical activity to appear and feel normally situated in the place of study, yet he or she must not lead conversation or direct behavior. Families can be asked directly not to alter their routines to accommodate the observer. Families must be confident that they are not being judged or evaluated by comparison to an external behavioral norm.

In research conducted in Wisconsin and California, observers participated in family routines for the duration of the observation periods. They ate with families, performed household chores, played with the children, and engaged in group entertainment, particularly television watching. A successful method for achieving rapport with family members during the second stage is for the observer to participate in activities that are important to each individual. For instance, ethnographers of dairy farm families should be prepared to help milk the cows, do the barnyard chores, assist in housework, and play with the young children. These behaviors help the observer become accepted by each member of the group. Such gestures should not be sustained to the point where they begin to interfere with the natural manner in which the activities are conducted. These moments of sharing labor have also proven useful for gathering additional information by means of informal questioning.

Validity and reliability checks on specific observations, concepts, behavioral rules, or theory are usually the last data-gathering responsibilities in family research. This third stage occurs after the last day of observation has been completed. Independent interviews are conducted with each family member. These question-and-answer sessions should be recorded on audiotape. They are unlike most other interviews in social research since by this time an unusual degree of rapport has been established between the observer and family members. This atmosphere contributes to relaxed, productive, and revealing interview sessions. During these sessions, family members are typically willing to comment at length about their feelings regarding the issues raised by the observer and to report their beliefs and opinions about other family members.

Organization and presentation of data

Three or four forms of raw data typically exist at the conclusion of the research period. Written materials include the notes taken by the observer during the time spent with individual families. The observer also has written a summary at the end of each observation day. Another form of written material sometimes used is a standardized interview schedule, administered to each family member during the final stage of data collection. Audiotape recordings are made by interviewing each family member at the conclusion of the observational period. Written transcripts are then made from the tape recordings. With these materials at hand, the ethnographer organizes and writes a report.

Written reports conform to one of three basic plans. First, if the ethnographer has studied family life with specific *a priori* research hypotheses in mind, the most effective way to report the findings is to organize the evidence around these hypotheses. In exploratory, interpretive, or phenomenological works, the report can focus on individual family members or on communications phenomena distilled from the raw data. Third, a combination of these approaches may be appropriate.

Some reports are book-length manuscripts. For instance, in one lengthy ethnography of family communication and mass media habits, each family was discussed in terms of its (1) family structure and communication patterns, (2) family media habits, (3) media habits of individual family members, and (4) particular communications phenomena including use of mass media to establish and demonstrate interpersonal dominance, parasocial interaction with television and the maintenance of marriage, television and exploration of interpersonal possibilities, natural viewing rights, regulation of program viewing, and successful role enactment (Lull 1976).

A simple but useful technique is to type all observational and interview notes that will be used in compiling the final ethnographic report. After carefully reviewing the data for themes to be explored in the analysis, observations and interview comments are sorted by first cutting the typewritten pages into units of one observation each. Then the researcher rearranges the bits of data into topics with the proper internal consistency in each.[2] Samples of conversation and descriptions of interaction patterns can be used to illustrate conceptual focal points. These data help the ethnographer of communication demonstrate the internal validity of areas to be developed theoretically. Finally, accurate and concise use of language facilitates ethnographic reporting, making the work credible and potentially useful to a wide range of readers.

OBSERVER OBTRUSIVENESS: SOME PERTINENT FINDINGS

A common criticism of ethnography is that the presence of an observer in a naturalistic environment must affect those who are observed, altering their behavior and thereby distorting the nature of the phenomena under study. The existence or magnitude of this problem has yet to be documented empirically; none the less, many researchers assume it to be true. Of course, every method of data collection is social research interferes in some way with the natural behavior of the individuals studied. In experimental or survey research, the investigator creates an unnatural event (the experiment with its artificial setting or the survey that solicits verbal recreations of reality). In ethnography, the investigator documents naturally occurring behavior but risks interference by being present.

In a study of audience members' uses of television, eighty-five trained observers were sent for three days into the homes of families unknown to them (Lull 1980b). Observations of family communication, including media use, were made the first two days. On the third day, the observer asked a standard set of questions of each family member seven years of age or older. The interview schedule included questions about possible effects of the observer's presence in the home.

Table 8.1 Was your behavior affected by the observer's presence?

	Yes	%
Fathers (n = 68)	14	20.6
Mothers (n = 82)	17	20.7
Children (n = 179)	48	26.8
N = 329	79	

Fathers and mothers were equally likely to say that the observer's presence affected their behavior (Table 8.1), with one of five indicating that they behaved differently. Children said they were only slightly more likely to be affected by the observer.

Family members reported three major categories of altered behaviors (Table 8.2). Most family members who said their behavior was different indicated that they were nicer, more polite, or more formal than usual. This finding may, in part at least, be due to the short period of observation in this study.

Family members more frequently believed that someone other than themselves was affected by the presence of the observer (Table 8.3). Generally, the person named as affected was one of the children. The child was usually said to be more animated or talkative, ploys apparently used to gain the observer's attention (Table 8.4). Respondents said the altered behaviors of other family members fell into three main categories: (1) animated attention-seeking talkative, (2) nice polite formal, and (3) shy nervous quiet inhibited. The reactions reported about other family members were similar to the behaviors that emerged from the self-reports.

Respondents strongly indicated that their television viewing was not altered because of the observer (Table 8.5). Parents and children both reported that, with few exceptions, their television habits did not differ with the observer in the home. This is an encouraging finding for ethnographers of audience behavior, because it indicates that even though some audience members modify their behavior with the observer present, these changes apparently do not involve the disruption of routine patterns of television use. In the few cases when television watching was reported to be altered, the distribution of changes revealed no systematic trend (Table 8.6). Among

Table 8.2 How was your behavior affected by the observer's presence?

	f	%
No difference	260	75.9
Nice polite formal	38	11.5
Animated attention-seeking talked more	12	3.6
Shy nervous quiet inhibited	16	4.8
Stricter	2	0.6
Talked to observer	4	1.2
Didn't specify difference	7	2.1
	329	100.0

the viewers who indicated that their amount of viewing changed, about the same number said they watched *more* television as *less* when the observer was in the home. Only two of the 329 who were questioned said that the television was turned off, on, or to a particular channel in order to accommodate the observer.

Table 8.3 Who acted differently?

	f	%	% (of individuals in subgroup)
Father (n = 68)	18	5.5	26.5
Mother (n = 82)	24	7.3	29.3
Child (n = 179)	87	26.4	48.6
Nobody	200	60.8	
	329	100.0	

Table 8.4 How did that person act differently?

	f	%
No difference	250	75.9
Nice polite formal	38	11.5
Animated attention-seeking talked more	12	3.6
Shy nervous quiet inhibited	16	4.8
Stricter	2	0.6
Talked to observer	4	1.2
Didn't specify difference	7	2.1
	329	100.0

SUMMARY

Ethnographic research is an interpretive enterprise whereby the investigator uses observation and in-depth interviewing to grasp the meaning of communication by analyzing the perceptions, shared assumptions, and activities of the social actors under scrutiny. This essay provides some specific practical suggestions for observing families in their homes. The recommendations are intended to illustrate particular approaches to studying the behavior of broadcast media audiences. These recommendations do not exhaust the possible ways of conducting family ethnographies, nor has every methodological issue been discussed.

Table 8.5   Was your television viewing different because of observer?

	Yes	%
Father (n = 68)	11	17.2
Mother (n = 82)	12	14.7
Children (n = 179)	22	12.3
	45	

Table 8.6   What were the differences in family television viewing?

	f	%
No difference	286	86.9
Watched more	18	5.5
Watched less	13	4.0
Watched different shows	1	0.3
Different viewer arrangement	4	1.2
Different viewer time	2	0.6
Advantage for child	2	0.6
More talk/activity	1	0.3
TV for observer	2	0.6
	329	100.0

Since ethnographic studies of audience behavior involve spending time in the natural environment where media messages are consumed, a discussion of the effects of the observer on family members has been presented. Data from a recent mass observation study demonstrate that the presence of the observer does not severely disrupt the normal behavior of families. Television viewing habits are infrequently disturbed under these conditions, and the changes that occur do not introduce any systematic bias.

NOTES

1   The idea of inconvenience may be stressed too strongly. In most cases, families say that they enjoy the presence of the observer. Many report

that they miss him or her when the observation period is completed. In some cases, lasting friendships have been made.

It may be useful at this time to ask the family to comment on the validity of the conceptual or theoretical structure that has developed during this process.

This chapter was originally published in Joseph Dominick and James Fletcher (eds) *Broadcasting Research Methods*, Allyn and Bacon, 1985.

REFERENCES

Bechtel, R., Achelpohl, C., and Akers, R. (1972) 'Correlates between observed behavior and questionnaire responses on television viewing', in E. A. Rubinstein, G. A. Comstock, and J. P. Murray (eds) *Television and Social Behavior, 4*, Washington, DC: United States Government Printing Office.

Cicourel, A. (1974) *Method and Measurement*, New York: Free Press.

Henry, J. (1965) *Pathways to Madness*, New York: Vintage Books.

Kantor, D. and Lehr, W. (1975) *Inside the Family*, San Francisco: Jossey-Bass.

Lewis, O. (1959) *Five Families*, New York: Basic Books.

——— (1965) *La Vida*, New York: Random House.

Lull, J. (1976) 'Mass media and family communication: an ethnography of audience behavior', doctoral dissertation, University of Wisconsin-Madison.

——— (1980a) 'The social uses of television', *Human Communication Research* 6, 3: 197–209.

——— (1980b) 'Family communication patterns and the social uses of television', *Communication Research* 7, 3: 319–34.

Madge, J. (1953) *The Tools of Social Science*, London: Longman, Green.

Meyer, T. P., Traudt, P. J., and Anderson, J. A. (1980) 'Nontraditional mass communication research methods: an overview of observational case studies of media use in natural settings', *Communication Yearbook 4*, Beverly Hills, CA: Sage Publications.

Reid, L. N. (1979) 'Viewing rules as mediating factors of children's responses to commercials', *Journal of Broadcasting* 23, 1: 15–26.

Wilkes, P. (1977) *Six American Families*, New York: Seabury/Parthenon Press.

Index